# 50 Money Making Ideas FOR Kids

adapted from materials by
## Larry Burkett
with Lauree and L. Allen Burkett
illustrated by Mark Herron

Tommy
NELSON™

Thomas Nelson, Inc.
Nashville

**50 Money-Making Ideas for Kids**

Concept by Lauree and L. Allen Burkett

Larry the Cat material adapted by Christie Bowler
Business ideas written by Marnie Wooding
Illustrated by Mark Herron

*For Money Matters for Kids*™
    Project Direction: Lauree and L. Allen Burkett

*For Lightwave Publishing*
    Managing Editor: Elaine Osborne
    Project Editor: Christie Bowler
    Art Director: Terry Van Roon

*For Tommy Nelson*™
    Managing Editor: Laura Minchew
    Project Editor: Beverly Phillips

Text and Illustrations
    ©1997 by Lauree & L. Allen Burkett.

Bible verses are from the *International Children's Bible, New Century Version,* copyright 1983, 1986, 1988 by Word Publishing.

**Library of Congress Cataloging-in-Publication Data**

Burkett, Larry.
    50 money-making ideas for kids
        p.   cm.
    Summary: Offers practical ideas for ways to make money during every season of the year, with quotes from Scripture and advice based on Biblical principles.
        ISBN: 0-8499-4045-1
        1. Money-making projects for children—Juvenile literature.
    2. Business—Religious aspects—Juvenile literature.
    3. Entrepreneurship—Juvenile literature.   [1. Money-making projects.   2. Business—Religious aspects.]   I. Burkett, Lauree.
    II. Title.
    HF5392.B87   1997                                    97-25841
    658.041—dc21                                              CIP
                                                              AC

*Printed in the United States*
97 98 99 00 RRD 9 8 7 6 5 4 3 2 1

# Contents

# Introduction

**Hi there!** Already I know some things about you! I know you're smart because you opened this book. Good move! So, you want to make some money! Great! Better yet, you want to know about business. See? I could tell you were smart.

Before you get started, there are a few things you should know. See, business isn't just about making money. And making money isn't just about money. Surprised? There are reasons for making money. Good reasons and bad reasons. You're interested in the good reasons. Right? Of course right.

**Why go into business and make money?** Because you want to make things better, change your world, and serve people (your customers or clients). Sound tough? It's simple. I'll show you. You make things better and people happy by providing a great product or fantastic service. As for changing the world, start small. You know: A way-cool drink on a hot day can change a grumpy face into a grinning face. A visit with your pet to a retirement home can change loneliness into happiness. Making people happy changes the world, person by person, grin by grin.

Remember the happiness of biting into that specially made hamburger with all the trimmings? Mmmm! And those fries. Yum! The restaurant made you happy by making a tasty product and serving it to you quickly for a decent price. That's good business, making the customer feel great.

**God made you to be like Him.** Ever notice that happy feeling you get when you've done an excellent job for someone? That's part of being like God. He made you to enjoy life, to love helping others, to be productive, and to have an impact on your world. He planned it so people (psst, that's you!) can serve the world and others around them. And guess what! Before you know it, you become the kind of person people want to be around. Why? Because you do things God's way; you work hard, have a good attitude about serving others, and do the best job you can. Things work out right when you go with God's plan!

**We're all part of a community.** See, your family's a community. Your school and church are communities. Your sports team, neighborhood, and scout group are all communities. Your mission is to find ways to serve these communities best. Don't forget your best is probably different from your buddy's best. You're unique! You have your own special gifts, interests, and talents. God made us all different. When each person does his or her own special "best stuff," the community is a happy and fun place to be.

Going on a camping trip? Don't get Absent-minded Annie to plan it or important things will stay behind. Try Plan-happy Patty. Best not let Mechanically-challenged Harry set up the tents. Let Tent-whiz Ted. You get the idea. Annie's great at organizing games, and Harry loves to cook. That's their part.

**Let's consider making money.** What is money? Little pieces of paper and bits of metal that people go ga-ga over. Why? Paper's not that valuable. But money's not just the paper, see. It represents something else—the value we give it. The government, shopkeepers, business people, and bankers all agree that those pieces of paper and metal have a certain value.

Now, there are basically two ways to get money. Your parents give it to you because you're part of their family. Or you earn it: You do chores or work for someone, and they pay you for it. Want to earn more? (Pay attention, this is important.) To earn more you can (1) work more hours or (2) make your time worth more by increasing your knowledge, skill, or speed. Simple.

**Here's how the system works.** You serve your customers by giving them something they need or want. They figure your work's worth money and pay you. You take that money and buy something you need. The seller uses the money you paid him for something he needs. Money travels from person to person and place to place. It's a medium of exchange: People exchange money for time, effort, products, or service. It's all part of being a community. Without your work some things wouldn't happen. Your customer wouldn't get great stationery. You wouldn't have money for new sports shoes. The shoe salesperson couldn't stay in business. The building owner where the shoe store is wouldn't get his rent. See the impact? Business is one great big chain! And it works! It makes the world go 'round. (Well, not really. The earth goes around anyway, but you get the picture.)

**Serve by giving.** Another way to serve your community is to give some of your money away. Giving to the church tells God thanks for all the stuff He's given you and for making you able to work. Also, give to people who are poorer than you—in this country or other parts of the world. That makes them happy, and it feels pretty good too!

Do you feel smarter? Only a few pages and already you know more about business and how money works. Wow!

**Now about this book.** There are oodles of money-making ideas in this book. We've arranged them by season. You know, summer, fall, winter, and spring. You're holding a year's worth of job ideas!

We've put a DIFFICULTY LEVEL with each idea. "**Easy**" means anyone 8 years old and up can do that job. "**Moderate**" jobs are good for kids 10 years old and up. "**Challenging**" jobs mean you should probably be 12 or older. (Hint: Do "older" jobs by getting more help.) We also suggest a REVENUE PRICE RANGE, but choose a price that works for your neighborhood and situation. (See pages 56-57, 100-101, and the form in the back of the book for help in pricing.)

We tell you how to get customers and give you ideas on how to make your business exciting and enticing. It's up to you to be smart and *learn all you can about your business.* You might have to buy other books, materials, and supplies. That's totally cool, and all part of the start-up cost of a business. For example, you can get gingerbread-house kits, books that give you a zillion kite-making designs, books on making balloon animals. . . . They help you make the product. We tell you how to sell it. What a deal!

Now you're almost ready to get out there and SERVE. But first, a bit more on this "business" thing.

# What Is Business?

You can be a business. You can do business. You can own a business. You can talk business. You can be the best in the business, and you can even stick to business. So what is business? A business is something you do (a service) or something you make (a product) that you sell to others. A house builder makes you a house (a product) and a security man protects your house (a service). These are both businesses. Sometimes you can join service and products.

Are you hungry? Let's have some lunch. Hamburgers, fries, and a soda pop sound good? Let's go order it.

The waiter who takes your order is doing a service. He or she is finding out what type of food you want and telling you how much it will cost. You pay and the waiter takes your money and then delivers your food to you. The waiter didn't make the food; he or she just serves it to you. You're right, that's a service.

Let's go in and check out the kitchen. The guy over by the grill is making your hamburger. He builds your lunch out of meat, lettuce, tomatoes, pickles, ketchup, onions, mustard, all on a sesame seed bun. He is making you a product. So the waiter and the cook have joined together to give you both a service and a product. They have a business!

What does our business do for us? Well, people pay for our services or our products. A business makes us money so we can have food, a home, clothes to wear, and money to buy things with and tithe to our church.

Getting into a business isn't easy. Sometimes we go to school to learn how to provide a service or product. We can also go to a business and ask employers to train us while we work. Learning about our jobs is the first step in doing well in that business whether we go to school or go straight to work.

It may cost you money to start your business too. You need some place to do your job. An office, store, or factory costs money to buy or rent. Equipment to do your job or make your product costs money too. A cook can't make your hamburger without a kitchen and a grill. Where you work, the equipment you use, and the supplies you need will all cost money. Remember, these are important things to know when you decide what to charge.

Before you start, there's an important question to ask yourself: Do people need your business? You better find that out before you start training and spending (investing) your money. Take my friend Utterly Unprepared. Utterly decided to sell snow boots to people living in the South American Rain Forest. He didn't sell very many boots because he forgot to learn about his business. You guessed it. It doesn't snow in the South American Rain Forest! It rains! Utterly was a poor business planner. He should have sold umbrellas. Smart planning makes for a totally, incredible, blow-your-mind-successful business.

You want another burger? Speaking of burgers. One snappy smart business guy is the Wendy's restaurants' Dave Thomas. He sells a lot of burgers by giving you good food, plenty of variety, and great service! Talk about a totally, incredible, blow-your-mind-successful business! There is a lot of stuff to remember when starting a business, but when you bring all these things to God in prayer and do it His way, things won't seem so hard. Your business should be God's business too.

# SUMMER

Yikes! Ouch! Ooooh, hot
sand, hot sand. Bare feet coming
through! Aaah. Cold water.
Going to the beach is great, but
summer can be more than
just that. If you're tired of beach
bouncing, come with me
and join the summer meltdown to
money-making madness.

# Flaming–Relish Hot Dog Stand

**1**

I am reporting live by satellite from the first Annual Lava Rock-Skipping Competition. This sport is hot! The contestants must skip their rocks across this bubbling pool of lava. Wait a minute! An unexpected problem has developed. It seems the rocks are melting instantly. The judges can't select a winner. Talk about disappointed athletes and heated fans! Back to you, Bob.

If you like hot stuff, try this cooking occupation. A hot dog stand might attract some attention at your next garage sale or church event. The day before your sale, take some of your savings or the money you've set aside for your business and buy the hot dogs, buns, and condiments. Store the wieners and other perishables in the refrigerator until needed. On the day, set up your hot dog stand with a bright tablecloth, napkins, and a sizzling sign with prices.

Have your parents help boil or barbecue the wieners. (Cook a few at a time. Be sure you don't make too many so they will be fresh for each customer.) At the stand, have your toppings ready in bug proof and easy to use containers. Allow your customers to select their own toppings to create a mouth-sizzling experience.

## Suggested Revenue
- $1.00 to $2.50 per dog.

## Tips
- Always wash your hands before you handle food. Money and food should never meet on your hands.
- You may want to sell cans of pop or juice as well.

## Tools
- Hot stuff: stand, sign, tablecloth, napkins, and money box with assorted change.
- Stomach satisfying: hot hogs, buns, mustard, relish, onions, and ketchup.

Don't have a molten meltdown when it comes to pricing. Be consistent.

---

## Business by the Book—
# Have Consistent Prices:

Deuteronomy 25:13—*Don't carry two sets of weights with you, one heavy and one light.*

We're not talking barbells! People used to sell things by weight. Some sellers carried around two sets of weights. With light weights they'd make it seem that the same amount of stuff weighed more. Then they would charge more. Price hike!

We don't weigh things today. But we might be tempted to change prices for different people. See a friend? For you, a special deal. That'll be $1.00. Oops, not selling enough or see a non-friend? Instant inflation. That'll be $2.00!

**Don't do it!** Set a price and stick to it. Customers will know if you change your prices. They'll feel cheated. Next time they'll buy from the competition, and you'll be left holding the dogs.

# Way-Cool Drink Stand

Phew! Are you hot? I mean sweaty behind the knees, sticky gum on the road hot? You could lay around counting lawn bugs, or how about selling cold drinks on a scorching day like this?

Where to put your drink stand? Being too far from the street is inconvenient for your customers. So, right on the edge of your lawn is the perfect location. But remember, don't block people from walking on the sidewalk, and especially don't block the road. Advertise! And not by yelling up and down the street like a maniac. Make a sign with balloons and streamers. Use words like *Cold*, *Refreshing*, and *Thirst-Quenching*. Don't forget to add the price.

Make your drinks look fancy (make them high-class or 'gourmet') by adding sliced fruit and ice. Keep them covered with plastic wrap. Use disposable cups to avoid having to stop and clean glasses and to show customers you keep a sanitary stand. You want your stand to be clean and your drinks to be fun and refreshing.

## Suggested Revenue
- $0.40 to $0.75 per glass.

## Tips
- Dress up like a tacky tropical tourist or clown to attract attention.
- Never leave your money by itself. Lonely money sometimes disappears.

## Tools
- Flashy sign stuff: poster board, paper, paint, felt pens, balloons, and streamers.
- Standard stand things: table, chairs, tablecloth, cups, napkins, money box with assorted change.
- Terrific tropical costumes.
- Gourmet ice tea or juice, ice cubes, and fruit.

Are there two drink stands on the street? Don't worry. If neighbor kids want to join in the fun, that's cool. Be partners! That's fair. Don't you think?

---

**Business by the Book—**
# Remain Debt Free:

Psalm 37:21—*The wicked people borrow but don't pay back. But those who do right give freely to others.*

Want to do right and give freely? It's hard to be generous when you have debts hanging over your head. Avoid them. Save up for what you'll need to begin your business before starting. It might take longer to get started, but you'll be debt-free.

If you have to borrow money, don't be wicked. Pay it back! Soon! Until you're out of debt, the money lender can ask for or take the money back anytime.

Avoid debts and be generous. Feels good to be debt-free, doesn't it? FREEDOM!

# Remote-Car Rally

I live to spin dirt, pick bugs from my headlights, and sneeze puffs of dirt! I'm a car-racing-rally radical. If you want to catch the speed, construct and start your own remote-control car off-road racecourse.

Monster trucks need some dirt-grinding action. If you have a piece of backyard that is perfect for developing an obstacle course, get into gear. Decide what type of obstacles you want: (a) a wheel-spinning dirt mountain (b) boulder-dodging slalom course (c) narrow-gorge bridge (d) spiraling-speed straightaway (e) hairpin curves (f) a gully gauntlet.

After you've finished construction, make a banner and some fliers to advertise. Have races every Saturday in the afternoon. Racers should bring their own cars, but have a couple of extra cars to rent just in case. Charge a fee for entry. Give small prizes for the winner of each round.

Purchase a few batteries to sell if car owners run low. Your friends will go totally turbo over this idea!

## Suggested Revenue
- $0.25 to $0.50 per run.

## Tips
- Have a free Grand Opening.
- Sell bags of chips and pop.
- Always keep the track in good condition.
- Change the course every now and then to make it more interesting.

## Tools
- Winning: wood bridge, shovels, rakes, rocks, bricks, fliers, banners, start and finish flags, prizes, snacks, radical remote-cars and trucks.

Make the best track you can and charge a fair price. If customers don't feel well–treated or don't get their money's worth, they won't be racing back. Doing the extra things will make your business a high-velocity victory.

---

**Business by the Book—**
# Have Integrity:

Proverbs 19:1—*It is better to be poor and honest than to be foolish and tell lies.*

If racers expect a boulder-dodging slalom racecourse but find a lazy Sunday afternoon drive, they'll roar their disappointment. Advertise what you have. If the truth isn't exciting enough, get to work. To bring the drivers you've gotta build the course.

Even if honesty means less sales, it's still the best policy. Think long-term. Mislead people now and they won't trust you later. Advertising the truth is a key to return customers. Give racers less than they expect? They're history. Give them more? They'll be back. With friends!

---

# The Wave Car Wash

Surf's up! Mud surfing is a very misunderstood sport. Brown oozing slime can be a turn-off for many athletes. Speaking of dirt, try this mud-busting car washing profession.

Car washing is best as a group activity. Get partners and make it a fun afternoon of suds and getting wet. On the day of your car wash post banners around the neighborhood advertising where, when, and how much. The location should be busy enough to attract drive-by customers.

Have a partner dress up in a clown suit, snorkel outfit (complete with flippers), or sandwich board (two signs joined at the top to form a sign tent). Stand near the road waving at cars, or try blowing lots of bubbles to attract attention. When the cars pull in, be ready by making sure windows and sun-roofs are shut tight and please don't get the car owner wet. Several people working on different parts of the car make the job go faster. Don't forget the roof and wheels!

## Suggested Revenue
- $5.00 to $8.00 per car.

## Tips
- You can't all do the same jobs. Let each partner decide what he or she is best at—like banner-making, cashiering, clowning, or car-washing. Switch halfway through.
- Take off heavy watches and jewelry so they don't accidentally scratch the paint.

## Tools
- Attention-getting props: banners, sandwich boards, balloons, streamers, costumes, and bubble wands.
- Serious washing equipment: hoses, buckets, sponges, car-safe detergents, and towels. (Don't forget the water.)

Group sports or jobs mean cooperation and having each person do what he or she is good at. It's like that in church, work, and play.

---

### Business by the Book—
# Be a Good Steward:

1 Corinthians 4:2—*A person who is trusted with something must show that he is worthy of that trust.*

Nothing you own is yours. Surprised? It's all God's. He just loans it to you to use. You're His "steward" or manager. Better take care of God's stuff, huh? God starts you off with small things. When you show you're worthy of His trust, He gives you bigger things.

You're the steward of your customers' property too. Treat it like it's a million bucks and soon you'll own a reputation worth that! Be a million-dollar steward!

---

# 5 Face-It Art

You don't have to be a major motion picture makeup artist to have fun creating wild characters and creatures. Face painting is one step toward movie magic. With a summer full of waiting little children you'll never run out of ideas or crew.

Set up a face-painting stand for a birthday party or church or school event. You could even set up at the beach. Parents and children might love some funny faces to complete their outing. You can purchase face paints and books at any craft, book, or novelty shop.

Make a light, portable sign to take on the road. Your sign should be bright and friendly, with sample photographs of faces you've already done, and prices. Bring along your books to look up ideas or put together a photo album of your own face creations. Be child-friendly by dressing up as an artist or funny creature. Remember, scary costumes will frighten small children and their sad faces would be harder to paint.

## Suggested Revenue
- $1.00 to $1.50 per face.

## Tips
- Bring along a silly hand puppet to make friends with nervous or shy customers.

## Tools
- Bright art supplies: face paint, brushes, makeup books, tissues, bowl of water, paint tray, and mirror.
- Amusing advertising props: silly photographs, photo album, balloons, costumes, hand puppet, and candy.
- Portable: chairs, table, sign, and mirror.

Roll tape and action! When you work with younger children, always be kind, friendly, and set a good example. Face it: You're their role model and maybe even their hero.

---

**Business by the Book—**
# Treat Others As You'd Like to Be Treated:

Luke 6:31—*Do for other people what you want them to do for you.*

Treating everyone with kindness and respect makes everyone happy.

How do you want to be treated? Want people to be nice to you, give you treats, listen to what you want, treat you like you're important?

That's how you should treat your customers. Find out what they want and give them as close to that as you can. Put in surprise extras. Your customers are important. Help them feel it. Guess what! They'll treat you nicely too.

# Just-Fooling Clowns

What is funny, silly, comical, goofy, crazy, laughable, zany, madcap, merry, weird, and totally wild (besides your brother or sister)? A clown! If you want to try clowning, get serious (not too serious) about this job.

Clowns don't joke when it comes to designing their costumes, makeup, and props. Take some time to decide what type of clown you want to be and how you want to look. Try different styles and funny character names. Work up an act by yourself or with friends. Clowns do everything from puppet or magic shows to juggling, acrobatics, and music, to just zany skits.

With a color photocopier or computer printer, make fliers with your clown photograph. Place them around your neighborhood, school, or church. Advertise that you'll do parties, school, church, or sporting events.

When clients call, give them a detailed description of what you will be doing. Arrive early in costume to set up. Don't let children see you putting on your costume; it spoils the illusion.

## Suggested Revenue
- $5.00 to $10.00 per hour.

## Tips
- Never go by yourself to a home or event you don't know or aren't familiar with. Have one of your parents go with you as an assistant or business manager. Parents could also help with keeping track of phone calls and clients.

## Tools
- Dazzlingly goofy stuff: costume, makeup, and props.
- Funny photograph and bright-colored fliers.

If you're feeling sad, unhappy, low, blue, and downcast, clowning around can make you feel totally goofy and happily bozo.

---

**Business by the Book—**
# Use Written Contracts:

Proverbs 22:3—*When a wise person sees danger ahead, he avoids it. But a foolish person keeps going and gets into trouble.*

People sometimes listen to the same words but hear different things. Misunderstandings. The Big "M."

As a business person, see the danger of misunderstanding up ahead and avoid it. How? Grab your pen, and write down what you'll do for the customers, when you'll do it, and how much they'll pay you. Sign it and get the customer to read and sign it. You now have a contract. If any misunderstandings come up, refer to your contract. Fight danger with your pen! Be wise.

---

# Cosmic-Characters Showtime Performers

I'm practicing for my act. I'm juggling one pillow feather, two watermelons, and three handfuls of mashed potatoes with butter while, you guessed it, standing on my head. Impossible? Come to the show and find out. Actually, why don't you start your own troop of wacky performers and join us?

Find out what weird and wonderful talents your friends have, and put on a show. Anything goes: juggling, magic tricks, funny plays, musical instruments, puppet shows, and pet tricks (maybe you can do one for your pet too). Entertain at parties, garage sales, school, sports days, Sunday school, and other community events. Each person should do at least a ten-minute act, so practice, practice, practice.

Dress in funny or eye-catching costumes. Before the show starts, have a short parade. Get people to follow you to your performance spot. Gather a crowd! One entertainer should be the announcer to introduce acts, and to open and close the show. Show performers usually put a hat down for money. Remember it is very important to thank everyone for their tips.

## Suggested Revenue
• Tips or $20.00 per performance.

## Tips
• Try to get the audience involved in the show. Ask volunteers to hold things, time tricks, or be a surprise character in a funny play.
• At the end of the show throw small candies out into the audience.

## Tools
• Totally cosmic: costumes, makeup, props, and small candies.

What an Act! Never hide any of the talents God gives you. So get out there and keep on shining.

---

### Business by the Book—
# Don't Book Too Far Ahead:

Proverbs 27:1—*Don't brag about what will happen tomorrow. You don't really know what will happen then.*

We're so good we're booked every night for 6 months! Aaagh! I forgot my sister's birthday, ball practice. . . . And now my cousins are visiting! My schedule book is so full I barely have time to say, "Nice to see ya!"

It's good to plan ahead and make commitments, but remember, a promise is a debt. If you promise to go somewhere, you gotta go! Even if it means missing a party. So only book shows a couple of weeks at a time. Leave space for surprises.

Only God knows the future. Put your future in his hands and leave some blank spaces in your book. Don't be a filled book, enjoy one!

# Ballistic-Balloon Base

I have my goggles, my cool dusty leather jacket, and this really weird long white scarf. Some pilots like their supersonic phantom jets or their mega powerful helicopters. I, on the other hand, prefer my balloons, especially with teddy bears and happy faces. You want to help sell some?

Balloon sales will go through the roof at parties, school, church, sport, or community events. First, get permission from the event organizers to set up your Ballistic-Balloon Base. Impressive!

With partners, create a solar looking balloon station. Dress up as a pilot or space person or in other cool costumes. Make and sell helium balloons and non-helium balloon animals. There are several books on how to create balloon objects. Practice so you can quickly make a number of different styles.

To make the helium balloons you first have to rent a helium tank from a party, rental, or novelty store. These tanks are hefty! Purchase a variety of string colors and balloon shapes. With an adult's help, just slip the balloon on the end of the tank nozzle and fill 'er up. Little customers will line up for miles.

## Suggested Revenue
- $0.50 to $1.00 per balloon; $1.00 to $2.00 per animal.

## Tips
- Four is a good number of helpers needed to: (a) fill up the balloons, (b) handle sales, (c) create balloon animals, and (d) walk around the event with a handful of balloons to sell.

## Tools
- Atmospheric: skinny animal balloons and strong helium balloons, string, helium tank, costumes, table, and cash box.

Working as a team is what makes a successful business fly, but choosing a good group leader helps the team with decisions, communication, and organization.

---

### Business by the Book—
# Pay Taxes:

Romans 13:7—*Pay everyone, then, what you owe him. If you owe any kind of tax, pay it. Show respect and honor to them all.*

Taxes. Everyone hates them. Everyone pays them. Everyone uses what taxes buy: roads, fire fighters, police officers, the army.

To run some businesses you need a license, and if you make over a certain amount you have to pay taxes. (Check the regulations in your state.) Then, at the end of the year you have to tell the government all about your business: Did you make a profit or lose money or buy lots of equipment? That's part of running a business.

So if your Ballistic-Balloons are a through-the-roof success and you owe the government taxes, pay up! Or never use a road again!

# Flashy Fruit and Vegetable Stand

Me Tarzan, you customer. I'm just hanging around my fruit stand. Hey! Has anybody seen a small chimpanzee and a big elephant? If you do, I'd move. They're not very good about waiting in line for their bananas. Do you want to do a produce stand too?

In the spring and early summer start planting your vegetables and fruit. Try corn, tomatoes, beans, strawberries, and small blueberry bushes. Have your parents help with the plant selection.

Or check out wild berry and vegetable picking, or go to a pick-your-own farm. Wash and dry your produce carefully so it's clean of dirt, mold, and (yuck!) bugs. You can purchase produce containers or plastic and paper bags. Price each package of fruit clearly so there is no confusion.

Can customers see your shop from the road? Make a sandwich board (two signs joined at the top to form a sign tent) for the road and a beautiful sign for your stand. Decorate with flower boxes, tablecloths, and maybe some country crafts. Keep your merchandise fresh by keeping it bug free and out of direct sun. Between sales, store your produce in a cool space. That's not just being picky.

## Suggested Revenue
• Price competitive with grocery stores.

## Tips
• NEVER eat or pick any wild fruit or vegetables until an adult says they're safe.

## Tools
• Gardening things: garden tools, seeds, water hose, and well-prepared garden site with rich soil and sunny location.
• Country goods: fruits, vegetables, table, tablecloth, signs, fruit containers, weight scale, flower boxes, decorations, and crafts.

No monkeying around. Running a store means investing a lot of time, planning, and energy. But hard work pays off.

---

### Business by the Book—
# Invest Your Money:

Ecclesiastes 11:2—*Invest what you have in several different businesses. You don't know what bad things might happen . . .*

Don't put all your hopes in one fruit basket—don't just sell one kind of fruit. Have several businesses (fresh fruit stands in winter are a bad investment).

Investing means planning for the future. Save your profits and put them into different things: your businesses, other people's businesses, education. . . . An investment makes money for you. If one investment doesn't give pay-back (good returns), another will. That way, if bad stuff happens, you're covered.

Make a good investment: yourself. Education, training, and great experiences will bring a big pay-back!

---

# See-You-Later Vacation Watch

Yes! Summer holidays! I've got my sunglasses, suitcase; and I'm on my way to sunny beaches, palm trees, and fun fruit drinks. While I'm away, why don't you try this vacation vocation?

While your friends, neighbors, or relatives are away, offer to Vacation Watch their home. Before your customers leave, make sure you have their house key, alarm system procedures, and phone number of where they'll be vacationing. Ask them to remind neighbors you'll be around.

Vacation Pet Watch. Walk, feed, clean cages, and keep their pets company once or, even better, twice a day. If you don't know the animal, go over for a visit. Take the animals for a walk (one at a time), give them a treat, or sit quietly with them. Make sure the owner writes a detailed description of dietary needs, health questions, daily routine, favorite activities, and their veterinarian's name and phone number.

Collect the mail and newspapers daily and pile them neatly in separate piles. Water plants according to your customers' instructions.

## Suggested Revenue
- $2.00 to $5.00 per day.

## Tips
- Keep an activity journal. Each day write down what chores and pet activities were done. Make note of any pet health or behavior problems and housekeeping accidents you feel are important.
- Keep house keys in a SAFE place and always double check locked doors and windows.
- Leave everything in as good or better shape than when your customers left.

## Tools
- Important food and tools should be provided by the home owner.
- For-the-record calendar or note paper for your daily journal.

---

### Business by the Book—
# Be Accountable:

Luke 16:12—*And if you cannot be trusted with the things that belong to someone else, then you will not be given things of your own.*

Be accountable. That means be ready to explain your actions to people. And they'll trust you because they know what you do.

Trust is kinda like a million bucks—hard to get and easy to lose, and you have to earn it. Start small and work up. If you can't look after a neighbor's dog, for example, why should your parents get you your own? You have to prove yourself.

So take care of things. Keep them in good repair and sparkling clean (feed, walk, and clean Fido the dog). And be ready to explain your actions when asked.

Soon you'll earn people's trust. And maybe the right to your own Fido, wagging tail and all.

---

# Pizzazz
# Picture Service

Freeze! Don't move a muscle, don't even blink. I've got you
covered. Now on the count of three. . . . One . . . two . . .
three . . . say CHEESE! If you want to get into the photo
phenomenon, click onto this business. When people forget
their cameras, have your photography service ready!

Do you own a Polaroid camera? Why don't you take it
with you to the next family, church, or school event? Offer to
take pictures! Just click, wait, and there you have it—instant
memories. Set one price for each picture (no matter how
many people are in the shot). Bring along silly costumes and
props. Get people to dress up and pose for funny pictures.
This is a great idea for summer birthday parties, family
reunions, church carnivals, and costume parties. If your
church or neighborhood has a summer fair, offer to take
pictures of competition or contest winners with their ribbons

and entries. Another great idea is to organize an owner and pet photo session. Have friends, family, and neighbors pose with their pets.

## Suggested Revenue
- $2.50 to $3.50 per picture; $3.00 to $7.00 per costume picture.

## Tips
- Please don't take someone's picture until you get his or her permission.
- Never force a customer to buy a picture he or she doesn't want, or one that didn't turn out well.

## Tools
- Photographer's getup: Polaroid camera with photo bag for carrying money and extra film.
- Crazy costumes and props.

Taking pictures that people like means understanding what they want. That isn't always easy. So stop, listen, and take the time to understand what your client wants.

---

### Business by the Book—
# Set Goals:

Proverbs 16:9—*A person may think up plans. But the Lord decides what he will do.*

You're going on a hike. Nice. How will you know when you get there? You need a destination (goal) or you'll never know. Okay, you're hiking to the top of Mount Olympus. Great! You need a destination in business too. Business goals. Say your goal is to go to camp. Now you know you need to take and sell enough pictures to cover the cost of your film and pay for camp.

But don't forget God's goals. Pray as you plan. Let God help you decide what to do. Following God is the greatest goal!

---

# Match Me to My Job

Hey neat, you can see my big toe! Time to get new shoes. Going to a Stanley's Super-Selection Shoe Store can be a little confusing. What a selection! They have flashing neon high tops, sandals, biking shoes, dress shoes, and way serious sports shoes. When you buy shoes you have to stop and decide: (a) Why you need them, (b) What types of things you'll be doing in them, and (c) What feels comfortable for you. (Remember, your friends can't try on your shoes for you.)

Okay. You seem to like those way serious sports shoes. Before you buy, stop and think! Do you do a lot of sports? Yes, you like sports. Hmmm. These shoes are expensive. Can you afford them? Yes, because you've carefully saved your money. Do you really need them? Yes! Coach says you're incredibly talented and to get better you'll need a good pair of shoes. In fact, you'll need them for the next big game, and today is the perfect time or opportunity to buy them. They fit perfectly. All right! Good job! You've carefully shopped. Your shoes and you will work together to win that big game.

Finding the perfect job match can be just as confusing as finding the right pair of shoes. There is a world of different and interesting businesses. It's important to stop and carefully consider a few points before you race into your career. Does your *personality suit the job* you're looking at? For example, if you don't like animals, becoming a veterinarian might not be the best job for you.

Do you have a *particular talent*? Someone who is awesome at singing might consider a career as a professional singer.

Has God given you *gifts that will help you* perform your jobs? A person who is gifted in, say, preaching and teaching the word of God may consider becoming a missionary. You're not sure you have gifts? Don't worry, you do. God will show you your gifts when the right time comes.

Do you have *an opportunity to do this job*? Opportunity means being able to do a business. You may want to mow lawns, and you bought a grass chopping, shredding, smashing, grinding, pulverizing lawn mower, but it's January and there's twenty feet of snow all over the place. No opportunity. But now, months later, you're walking through waist-high grass in the middle of summer. But you've sold your grass chopping, shredding, smashing, grinding, pulverizing lawn mower. No opportunity again! I'd say it's time for some sit-down opportunity planning. Don't you?

Can you *physically do the job* you want to do? Say you want to be a captain of a naval destroyer, but you get sick every time you get on a ship. Not good. This job just doesn't suit you.

Why do we have to think of all these things? Well, you don't want to be stuck in I-don't-like-my-job quicksand! God wants us to be happy in the things we do, including our jobs.

Remember your shoes? You don't buy a pair of shoes without careful shopping. Don't do that with a business either.

Take your time, shop around, and try on a few job ideas before you commit to one. Bring your business future to God in prayer. That's just running with a smart career planner. Together you'll find the perfect fit and score in the big world of business.

# FALL

Hold on! I've got something to show

you. Here, hold out your hand.

I went for a walk and got some pretty

interesting stuff. Let's see, some nifty

rocks in one pocket and in the other

a whole bunch of autumn leaves,

a dozen snail shells, and some

squishy cocoons. Fall is the time to

go out and collect neat nature stuff.

Why don't you gather up these

autumn business ideas too?

# 12

# To-the-Point Personalized Pencils

Yes siree! I'm up to my elbows in craft glue because I've been working so hard gluing, wrapping, and having some fun. If you like decorating, try making personalized pencils.

The beginning of the school year is the perfect time to sell your pencils. Get permission from your teacher or principal to do your selling at lunch or recess. Dressing up pencils or pens is easy to do with a few craft supplies and a lot of imagination: (a) Wrap Pencils. Wrap and glue colorful embroidery floss around a pencil or pen to create a rainbow and add feathers to the pencil end as well! (b) Creature Pencils. Hot glue pompoms on a pencil end to make fuzzy bunnies, bears, and monsters. Add goggle eyes, pipecleaners, and other things to make them look even better. (c) Sticker Pencils. Easy! Just press interesting stickers securely all around the pencil. (d) Papered Pencils. Hot glue gift wrap, wall, or craft paper around a pencil. (e) Named Pencils. Do the customer's name in fancy letters.

Don't forget to make theme pencils for parties, holidays, and other special events.

## Suggested Revenue
- $1.00 to $2.00 per pen or pencil.

## Tips
- Your decorations shouldn't interfere with sharpening and holding the pencil.
- Your class can make personalized pencils as a gift for the new teachers and other students in your school or Sunday school. Then take orders for later sales.

## Tools
- Perfect project stuff: pencils, glue, embroidery floss, pompoms, pipecleaners, goggle eyes, decorative paper, and stickers.

Before you spend all that fancy city money make sure you don't owe Mom or Dad for any of the craft materials. Paying bills is just down-home smart.

---

**Business by the Book—**
# Pay Your Bills:

Romans 13:8—*Do not owe people anything. But you will always owe love to each other. The person who loves others has obeyed all the law.*

Every duck has a bill. Every business has bills. It's a fact of life. Business and bills go together like dentists and teeth, school and teachers, home and chores.

Successful businesses have paid bills. Your local craft store might give you credit, but that just means you pay the bill later.

The only things you should owe for any length of time are terrific things like love, kindness, and friendship.

So be a good duck and have only one bill: love.

# 13

# Likable Laces

In fifty seconds I, the Amazing Escapeo, will remove these
handcuffs, untie these incredibly tight ropes, unlock titanium
padlocks, pry open this chained sea trunk, and, finally, swim
thirty feet through piranha-infested waters to complete my
thrilling escape act. Starting now! And speaking of Amazing
Escapeo being tied up, you can get tied up in this fun
business idea while you're waiting for his great escape.

Make and sell fancy shoelaces. Your friends will think
they're cool, and craft-fair customers will buy them by the
pairs. With fabric dyes and beads you can create brilliant
laces. To get a crazy multi-colored tie-dyed look, use several
dyes and dip your laces any which way you like. Use holiday
colors for Christmas, Easter, Valentine's Day, and Saint
Patrick's Day.

To add to the fun, purchase wild beads or buttons and
thread them on! Search through craft stores for holiday
accessories like bunny-, heart-, and angel-shaped beads—and

dinosaurs. Thread or tie them on. Summer, spring, winter, and fall can all have their own special colors and beads.

## Suggested Revenue
- $1.50 to $3.00 per pair.

## Tips
- Different shoes or sports can be a theme as well: hiking boots, in-line skates, ice skates, and dance shoes. For example, hiking-boot laces might have earthy colors and animal or wood beads.
- Check out craft stores for interesting beads.

## Tools
- Wacky laces, fabulous fabric dyes, and wild wonderful beads and buttons.

Before you start a business, always research and make sure you understand exactly what you'll be doing, or how to make and sell a good product. If you don't, you may wind up in over your head and stuck in a trunk like me. Is anyone still out there?

---

### Business by the Book—
# Be Fair:

James 2:9—*But if you are treating one person as if he were more important than another, then you are sinning.*

You know the kids everyone wants to be friends with? Yeah, Susy Sizzle and Huey Hotshot. Well, here they come! They're stopping at your booth. Wow! You've always wanted to be their friend! What do you do?

Nothing special. You do exactly what you do for Sheila Shyness and Michael Mild. Everyone gets the same treatment. They pay the same price and get the same smile. You see, everyone's equally important and equally fine. So if you give Suzy and Huey special treatment, best give Sheila and Michael the same.

Don't sin by favoritism. Be fair.

---

# 14

# Write-Stuff
# Personalized Stationery

When you're orbiting a thousand miles above the Earth in a tiny space ship, mail delivery isn't very good and postage is outrageous. If you have Earthly pen pals, or know people who just love to write letters, personalized stationery sure delivers a great letter.

You can make unique stationery by dressing up the borders of blank paper and envelopes. Sell them at craft fairs, consignment gift shops, school, or church. Stationery with a theme is terrific. Make them for the holidays: (a) For Christmas stationery use holiday stamps and green or red ink. (b) For Easter, stenciled flowers painted over sponge-painted borders look pretty. (c) Valentine's Day may have lace and heart-shaped hole punches with threaded ribbon. (d) Make Summer holiday stationery with blue marbleized edges. Add sailboat and seashell stickers. The ideas are endless.

You can make stationery for special groups too: dog shows, boat clubs, horse shows, gardening clubs, or music societies. Customers will go crazy over stationery designed just for their interests.

## Suggested Revenue
- $3.00 to $6.00 per set of ten.

## Tips
- Take orders and put individual names or initials on stationery with gold stamps or fancy calligraphy (handwriting). Take a calligraphy class and practice.
- Make an album displaying your stationery themes and decoration techniques.
- Buy stationery paper at craft and stationery stores.

## Tools
- Elegant crafts: paper, envelopes, paints, stamps, ink pads, stickers, hole punches, glue, glitter, ribbon, lace, ink, brushes, pens, sponges, and a whole bunch of other amazing things.
- Self-decorated sample album.

When we write letters to people, we take time out of our busy day to think about them. Don't forget to stop and do the same thing for Jesus.

### Business by the Book—
# Have Integrity:

Proverbs 13:6—*Doing what is right protects the honest person. But evil ruins the sinner.*

Want top quality protection? No, don't hire a bodyguard. Be honest!

Have integrity—doing what you say, doing it well, and never cheating anyone or skimping on delivering what you promise, are great ways to stay safe. Sell only your best fancy stationery. Count the papers accurately—and add a couple for good measure. Give people what they ask for. If you goof on some pages, have a discount section for imperfect stationery! Such a deal! People will love buying from you.

So get protected! Be a person of integrity!

# 15

# Don't-Get-Bored Job Ideas

Psst. Hey you! Yeah, you! Come here. I've got something to ask you. Are you bored? I'm not joking. By the way you're twirling your gum around your finger, I figured you were bored. Am I right, or am I right? Okay, I've got the solution. But don't be telling anyone else, see. Because they might want in on the action.

Get the Big Bosses. You know, your parents. Yeah, I said your parents. Ask your parents to make a Job Board. What's a Job Board? Are you wet behind the ears or what? Your parents make a list of extra jobs around the house that need doing. And you do them and they pay you. No big deal, but don't think you can weasel out of your regular duties because that's not the way the deal works. You do some jobs because you're part of the family. These are extra jobs. Get it?

You could do chores like washing the car, mowing the lawn, or painting the fence. Whatever the Big Bosses want. Every week ask the Bosses to put up a new list with prices. A beautiful arrangement, if you ask me. Don't forget to do a good job every time, because we'll be watching.

## Suggested Revenue
• What the Big Bosses want to pay.

## Tips
• Do regular chores before the extra paid jobs.

## Tools
• The job list and the Big Bosses' tools.

I know you're going to be overjoyed with the loot you're going to make each week. But don't be a wise guy. A smart kid like you knows to give 10 percent of what you make to your church as a tithe.

---

### Business by the Book—
# Tithe:
Proverbs 3:9—*Honor the Lord by giving him part of your wealth. Give him the firstfruits from all your crops.*

You're a business person, not a farmer? No crops? Call your business your crop. The first money you make goes to God. That's what "firstfruits" means. Remember it's all His anyway. You're just His manager. So give a tithe, 10 percent, back to His church.

Tithing reminds you that what you have is just on loan. It tells God you agree it's all His. Can't afford it? Wrong. That's when you really need to tithe. Don't worry. God'll look after you. He's real generous. There's just no way to out-give God.

---

# 16

# Leaf-It-to-Me Leaf Raking

Gravity 53 . . . gravity 54 . . . gravity 55! . . . OUCH! What am I doing? Picking apples, of course, but they always seem to fall on my head. Apples and gravity just kind of go together, sort of like autumn and a leaf-raking business.

Notify your seasonal customers that you will be available to rake leaves. Attract new customers by placing a flier in your local garden shop's window or bulletin board. Include your name, phone number, price, and perhaps a list of signatures from past satisfied customers.

Bring your own gardening equipment, so you know it is in good condition, and your own garbage bags. Don't forget to rake around and under shrubs. Be gentle around small bedding plants so you don't damage them. For an extra fee, offer to clean leaves from pools and ornamental ponds.

## Suggested Revenue
- $5.00 to $6.50 per hour.

## Tips
- If your customer has a fall fruit tree or other fall crops, offer to harvest it.
- Another extra service might be fall bulb planting. The customer supplies the bulbs, fertilizer, and planting plan. You supply the muscles.
- After a BIG wind storm, phone your clients and tell them you are available to clean up fallen tree branches and other wind related yard problems.

## Tools
- Professional flier material: paint, felt pens, leaf stamps, computer, and autumn tinted paper.
- Muscle building: rakes, shovels, wheelbarrow, garbage bags, and pond strainers.

Part of being reliable in business is anticipating (looking out for) your clients' needs and being there to get the job done. Unlike gravity, don't let your customers down.

## Business by the Book—
# Be Reliable:

Deuteronomy 23:23—*You must do whatever you say you will do. You chose to make a promise to the Lord your God.*
Promises to customers are like promises to God: a must to fulfill. So only promise what you can deliver. Promise a customer "You have leaves; I'll rake." Then you need to show up on time with rake in hand!

Leaves raked aside, being reliable is about character, reputation, trust, and success. Become known as a kid who keeps his word, or a kid who's always there when you need her. That reputation can get you repeat customers, extra jobs, references, tips, letters of recommendation. . . .

Be as reliable as the falling fall leaves.

# 17

# Almost-a-Marathon Dog Walking and Grooming

One dog went left, the other went right, and this little tiny crazy Chihuahua just ran around and around. Now we're tied together, and this St. Bernard is sitting on my foot. Take the lead and start a pet service of your own.

Do you know busy or elderly pet owners in your neighborhood? Find out if you could walk and groom their pets. Offer to pet walk once or twice a day for a weekly fee. Get a couple of friends to join the business and make it a pet walking club. Always arrive at your client's house on time and, if you can't walk that day, phone. Don't forget to bring a small shovel and plenty of plastic bags, because a responsible pet walker always cleans up.

Pet grooming could be done weekly. Pet grooming isn't just for dogs. Long-haired cats, rabbits, and guinea pigs need a good brushing too. Use your client's grooming equipment so you don't spread fleas from pet to pet. If you notice fleas, ticks, or anything unusual, notify the owner immediately. Get permission to offer a pet treat after each grooming.

## Suggested Revenue
- $1.00 to $3.00 per walk.

## Tips
- Always keep the dogs on their leashes and never walk more than one dog at a time. You don't want fights.
- If a pet constantly misbehaves, don't work with that animal.
- If a pet seems cranky or unwell, skip the grooming and try another day.

## Tools
- Pampering pet treats and necessary small shovel and plastic bags.

Let kindness, safety, and fun be a big part of your service. After all, pets are friends for life!

---

## Business by the Book—
## Serve Others:

Mark 10:43—. . . *If one of you wants to become great, then he must serve you like a servant.*

"Pet servant becomes hero!" Who would have thought you could get ahead by serving? Well, God did! It's a mystery. But being a good servant to customers, friends, teachers, family . . . everyone, makes them feel like heroes. That makes you a hero.

Service is an attitude that comes from the heart. If it's faked over gritted teeth, people and pets know it. They'll growl right back. Serve from the heart. Make it your goal to treat your customers like royalty. Make them feel special. Be a hero!

---

# 18

# Don't-Junk-It Recycling Service

It took three hundred tin cans, twenty old tires, one hundred broken computer parts, and two lawn mower engines to create the most amazing technological and environmentally friendly robot the world has ever seen. What does he do? Well, so far, if you knock him over he squashes cans. If you're into the environment, re-use this out-of-the-dumps occupation.

It takes a lot of time and muscle to recycle household papers, cans, bottles, and scrap metals. Sometimes elderly people have a hard time sorting through their recyclables. Advertise at seniors' community centers that you will sort garbage and pack recyclables. If your city has a recycling pick-up service keep track of your clients' pick-up days on a calendar. On the pick-up morning, take out their garbage and recyclables. If there is no pick-up service, offer to take their recyclables to the depot every two weeks.

Add a composting service as well. Offer to build and maintain your client's garden compost. Once a week, turn the compost and remove any other yard waste. Whenever needed, spread the new soil around the garden.

## Suggested Revenue
- $2.00 to $3.00 curb-side service per week; $10.00 to $15.00 per depot run; $5.00 per hour compost service, not including construction material.

## Tips
- Start your own worm compost. Find out the facts about worm composting from your community recycling program. Worms are at home in apartments, offices, and schools too!

## Tools
- Environmentally friendly: muscles, shovels, compost building material, worms, and lots of recyclable material.

Keeping the world God created healthy is an important job. Be the top of the heap when it comes to recycling, re-using, and keeping our environment clean.

---

### Business by the Book—
# Be a Good Steward:

Genesis 1:28—*God blessed them and said, 'Have many children and grow in number. Fill the earth and be its master.'*

There are lots of people filling the Earth nowadays—not many mastering it. It's a big job, but someone's gotta do it. (That's why you started this business, right?) Step right up, roll up your sleeves and get mastering.

God gave us the job of caring for our planet—keeping it safe and healthy, and looking after the various critters (people too) that live here. So grab your cans, papers, and bottles and put them where they'll do the most good.

Earth Master to the rescue!

---

# 19

# Total-Action-Sports-Assistant Hero Person

Is it a bird? Is it a plane? Is it the coach? No, it's Total-Action-Sports-Assistant Hero Person! There are many sports–related jobs that Total Action Hero People can do.

Do you play a team sport? Find out about referee schools. Some sports allow boys and girls to start referee training at eleven or twelve. You can earn good money each weekend by refereeing peewee games.

Assisting the coach during the season or during summer sport schools is another good idea. A busy coach of a peewee team would be glad to have help setting up and putting away equipment, and running drills.

Being a golf caddy for your parents and their friends on the weekends and after school is an excellent part-time job.

## Suggested Revenue
• Trade for services.

## Tips
• Payment isn't always money; you could work for extra coaching help as well.

## Tools
• Completely impressive resume and letters of reference.
• Your sport's sports equipment.

Even superheroes take time off. Juggling school, jobs, and free time isn't always easy. Working hard is important, but so is having fun.

---

### Business by the Book—
# Have Balance:

Psalm 127:2—*It is no use for you to get up early and stay up late, working for a living. The Lord gives sleep to those he loves.*

Don't be a workaholic. Or a playaholic. Balance is the key. Ask any high-wire artist.

Don't get caught up in making money. Get caught up in life.

God worked. God rested. He told us to work and rest. Life isn't all school, homework, and chores. But it's not all sports, play, and fun either. It's a little of both. And family, friends, and God.

God looks after the people He loves. That's you! Do your part, then relax. God'll take care of the rest.

Walk the high-wire. Live with balance.

---

# 20

# Computer Overdrive

Where are you going, pal? Wait, I've got a few questions to ask you. Are you computer crazy? Are you keyboard sly? Are you the household hacker? If you are, push ENTER. Do you have little brothers and sisters or even parents and grandparents that don't quite seem to get computers? Become their teacher and pathfinder into the information highway.

Are you learning about computers at school or even on your own with books and programs? Ask your parents if they will pay you to teach your younger brothers and sisters, or pay you to help monitor their Internet explorations. Don't be surprised if your grandparents or great-grandparents might love the chance to try this new technology with your help.

Remember, make the computer educational and fun. Set aside an hour once or twice a week for each student. Plan your lessons in advance! Plan what your students will learn that session, and what programs or skills you want them to try. If they are having problems, don't step in too quickly. Part of the adventure is letting the students try on their own.

## Suggested Revenue
- $4.00 to $7.00 per hour.

## Tips
- For junior hackers, make a chart with reward stickers, or let them try a new fun game program.
- Trade your teaching services for new programs or other wished-for computer equipment.
- When teaching adults, don't forget to have extra patience and lots of respect.

## Tools
- All necessary technical computer equipment.
- Rewards: poster board, stickers, or game programs.

Teach self-confidence and pride too! You don't want your students to be pushing ESC halfway through your lesson because they feel confused, dumb, or pressured.

---

### Business by the Book—
# Honor Authority:

Ephesians 6:5—*Slaves, obey your masters here on earth with fear and respect. And do that with a heart that is true, just as you obey Christ.*

Crack the whip! No. You're the slave. Your students are the master. You live to serve your customers. And adults are to be honored (respected) and obeyed at all times.

Your job is to give customers what they pay for. That's what a business does: It meets a need and offers a service. But that service must be given respectfully from the heart to all your wanna-be hackers. Respect. Patience. The keys to happy customers. They might just recommend you to other wanna-bes.

# Planning

I'm going on a trip to visit some missionaries in Uganda, Africa. Whenever you go somewhere, you should plan ahead. It will be hot. I'd better pack my sunglasses and sunscreen. I know how long I'll be staying, so I can pack just the right amount of clothes.

Planning a business is a lot like planning for a trip. When you choose your business, you'll want to make sure you have all the equipment you need.

I buy my airplane ticket weeks ahead of time so I can leave the day I want to. A business manager is organized and well prepared too. He or she knows what supplies or travel plans the company needs weeks or months before they'll need them.

Before I leave, I contact my friends in Uganda to make sure they can meet me at the airport. That's smart travel planning. When you start a business, you want to make sure you'll have customers. You can advertise your business or contact people you know who will be interested in your service. That's smart business planning. You don't want to be waiting for customers all by yourself.

I studied some of the local languages and the way they do things in Uganda. I'll need to learn all about the country, animals, and environment. Learning the business skills you need is important too! Train yourself, and know your business stuff!

Without careful planning my trip wouldn't get off the ground, and it wouldn't be a success. With careful business planning you'll have the knowledge, equipment, and customers to make your company fly. I'll be able to say Hujambo (greetings) to my friends in Uganda, and you'll be able to say hello to new customers.

# What to Charge

My name is Thomas. Today my big brother got a new skateboard. Maybe he'll sell me his old board. Can you believe it? He wants thirty dollars! That's not fair. If I had an old skateboard, I'd sell it to him for way less. Mom said I should put a notice up on the school bulletin board saying I want to buy a used skateboard. I put up a notice, and guess what? I got a really great board for ten bucks! Cool!

When you sell a product or a service you have to consider both how much money you want to make and how much money your customer will spend. Big brother might have wanted thirty dollars, but his customer wasn't willing to pay that amount. Thomas shopped around and found the deal he wanted.

A business manager wants to cover all her expenses when deciding her prices. Remember to use the budgeting form to help with your price calculations. A manager wants to cover her time, supply cost, her employees' salaries, and she wants to make a profit. But if covering all those things means her product or service is too expensive, customers won't buy and her business won't be a success. Businesses have to stay competitive by keeping their prices down so people will do business with them instead of other similar companies. When you start a business, find out what other companies charge for their product or service. Decide if you can afford to charge the same amount or less. You have to price fairly, and still make a profit. Thomas was happy, and so was the skateboard seller. When both sides are satisfied that makes for good business.

# WINTER

*One . . . two . . . umph . . . three . . .*

*four . . .* What am I doing? . . .

*five . . .* Sit-ups! Why?

I'm training for the Winter Olympics!

*. . . six . . .* ! But not the kind you

think. Job Olympics. Winter is where

it's at when it comes to starting a

business. And staying in shape

is part of it *. . . seven . . . eight . . .*

Check out these really cool

winter ideas.

# Headline–Banner Bonanza

Mount Everest! I've made it to the top! But I need proof. I know, a banner! Sometimes for special occasions people use big signs or banners to announce things like birthdays or community events. If you know anyone celebrating something or organizing an event, ask them if you could make a banner in exchange for money, free entrance tickets, or maybe sale items. Confusing? Not at all.

Let's use your neighbor Mr. Bargain as an example. Mr. B is having a Christmas tree sale. He wants lots of people to buy his trees. But has he done enough advertising? Enter Banner Hero! (Psst, that's you.)

Make several big sale banners and place them around the neighborhood to catch people's attention. (Your parents can help you find out if there are any city fees or size limits.) Make them colorful with big lettering so people can read them clearly from a distance. Staple your banner to wood support poles or tape it securely to other objects like houses or between trees. Never place your banners on someone else's property without asking, and never cover up street or business signs. Remember! It is your job to remove your signs. Don't leave them for other people to take down.

## Suggested Revenue
- $5.00 to $15.00 per big banner; $6.00 per front and back sandwich board; $3.50 to $5.00 for walking advertising.

## Tips
- Construct a sandwich board! You know, a sign on your front, and another at your back attached by string on your shoulders. Wear it while you and a friend walk around your neighborhood advertising the sale.

## Tools
- Supplies: paper, paints, and felt pens.
- Extra-sturdy support poles and tape.
- Sandwich board gear: white cardboard and string.

Mr. B is impressed. Congratulations. We don't wear real banners on us every day, but our behavior and the things we do tell people about us.

---

### Business by the Book—
# Be Diligent:

Proverbs 22:29—*Do you see a man skilled in his work? That man will work for kings. He won't have to work for ordinary people.*

Want to brush up against royalty? Be the best: No ordinary Banner Hero, but a Banner Superhero! Doing your best is the key to impressed customers. Impressed customers are the key to a successful business. And that's the key to spreading the word. How else will royalty know?

So craft every banner into a Great Banner: Make it a work of art, a poem, an eye-catcher, a one-of-a-kind, draw-the-customer-in masterpiece.

You'll be invited to do more. Your work will be in demand! Word will spread! SOON, KINGS WILL CALL!

---

# 22

# Too-Sweet Candy Company

Should I or shouldn't I? What if I bite into it and find out I don't like it? Maybe I will, but maybe I won't. I hate making decisions. Especially about chocolates. Hey, if you like candy too, this just might be the perfect business for you. From fudge to taffy, cookies to lollipops, there are a number of treats that are easy to make.

The library is a great place to explore candy making books. Have your parents help you with heating the chocolate for shaped chocolate pieces. All you have to do is heat the chocolate, pour it into purchased candy molds, and cool.

Taffy pulling with a friend is hilarious fun, and it makes lots of candy!

Tie up pretty bundles of candies in colored cellophane and ribbon, or make fruit basket cages and fill with pretend chocolate covered bugs. Take a boxful to church or school.

Remember to get permission from your teacher, principal, or minister. Ask if you can sell your candy on Valentine's Day or other special days at recess, lunch time, or after church. Give a percentage of the money you make to help fund school projects or to contribute to a missionary fund.

## Suggested Revenue
- $1.50 to $4.00 per bundle, including delivery.

## Tips
- For fun, add free delivery to your candy parcels. While one person handles sales, a partner can deliver the candy to a friend the customer chooses, in the church building or school grounds only.

## Tools
- Candy ingredients.
- Kitchen stuff.
- Bright colored cellophane and ribbon.

I finally decided which candy to choose. Mmmm, caramel. Just what I hoped it would be.

---

### Business by the Book—
# Give:

Proverbs 11:25—*A person who gives to others will get richer. Whoever helps others will himself be helped.*

Wanna be rich? Give stuff and money away! No, don't choke on your candy. There's more to riches than money. You can be rich in friendship, character, and a heart that cares. Those riches last past the swallow.

So give things away. Put extra candy in the bags. Donate money to charities or missions. Share with others. You don't lose by doing this. You grow richer in the things that count.

Giving to people makes them feel rich. They'll come back for more and make you rich with friendship and coins.

---

# 23

# Dynamite Decorations

I'm hanging upside down in this Christmas tree. How did I get up here? It's a long story involving a South American iguana, a cat, and a piece of tinsel. While I get down, why don't you start your own holiday decoration service?

How about doing some holiday decorating for a small fee? There are so many holidays during the year this business just keeps popping up on your calendar. For Christmas you could decorate trees, make Christmas wreaths, or help an adult untangle and put up outdoor lights. Easter's the perfect time to dress up baskets or make paper flowers. Be a secret Valentine admirer by making hearts and ribbons to brighten your customers' houses. Your Fourth of July flags and banners will be the hit of the block party. Thanksgiving tables won't be complete without your autumn table centerpiece. The neat thing about decorating is that anything goes and it's so fun!

## Suggested Revenue
• $1.50 to $15.00 per creation.

## Tips

- Make a special surprise card or decoration for each member of your family, or a customer's family. Hide them and have a holiday hunt.
- Don't forget to include taking down and packing decorations as part of your service.
- Larger crafts, like wreaths, cost more to make. Remember to charge enough to cover the cost of your materials!

## Tools

- Seasonal decorations, baskets, paper, glue, ribbon, paints, felt pens, autumn leaves, pine cones, and an endless amount of other craft supplies.

Being good at our jobs is something to be proud of, but we don't want to brag about it. Bragging doesn't make us look good. When we do something the way God wants it done, people will notice without our having to say anything about it.

---

**Business by the Book—**
## Be Humble:

Philippians 2:3—*When you do things, do not let selfishness or pride be your guide. Be humble and give more honor to others than to yourselves.*

Humble pie! Mm-mm-good! Fruity and spicy with a nice tang. Let others feast on praise while you enjoy a nice light snack.

Work (decorate) so people will have beauty, not so you'll get applause. Make sure your team members or helpers get recognition for their parts. Don't worry about your own recognition. It's nicer to work with someone who thanks you than someone who makes you thank them!

Consider money a big bonus! Do your work for joy; for the looks on their faces, for the smiles and eye-crinkles that say, "Wow. That's beautiful!" That flavor of appreciation soaks in to the toes. It's great!

# 24

# Dig-It
## Snow Removal

It's winter. I've got my hat. I've got my gloves. I've got this gigantic snow shovel, and I'm wearing seven layers of clothes. I'm really ready. Did I mention that what I don't have is snow?

Even before the first snowfall of the year you can prepare for your first day of business. In the fall you could make up fliers advertising that you will be shoveling walkways in the winter. Giving people, or as we in the Biz call them, "clients" or "customers," early notice will help them remember you and will demonstrate that you plan ahead. Decide in advance how many people you want to notify, so you don't make too many copies of your flier.

When clients do call, give them an exact time you will be there. Keep track of who the clients are, where they live, and when you will be at their homes. Remember to space your appointments apart so you won't feel rushed and can do a good job for each client.

If customers recommend you to someone else, be sure to give them a little discount the next time you shovel their walks. This shows you appreciate their recommending you and makes them feel good about doing business with you.

## Suggested Revenue
• $4.00 to $6.00 per hour.

## Tips
• Clear the paths completely and pile the snow neatly away from small shrubs so the weight of the snow doesn't damage them.

## Tools
• Brilliant fliers.
• Gigantic snow shovel.
• Awesome muscles.

Well, I'm still waiting for that snow. But I planned ahead, and I'm ready to start my business. And that's not flaky.

---

## Business by the Book—
# Plan Ahead:

Proverbs 6:6, 8— . . . *Watch what [the ants] do and be wise. . . . they store up food in the summer. They gather their supplies at harvest.*

Be an ant: Carry off bits of food. Oops. I mean: Plan ahead.

Prepare for winter work in the fall. It's good for business. Clients believe that someone who plans ahead will be ready, organized, and reliable. And they're right. Customers want reliable workers so they can plan things too.

Let them know you and your snow shovel will be available. When the white stuff falls, they will call. And you'll be carrying off snowflakes to the great ant-hill on the side.

# 25

# Snow–Fun Sitters

Burrrrrr it's cold! Hyper-hibernation is more my thing. But, if you crave the cold, try this polar occupation. Little children love to play outside on a snowy day. Unfortunately, parents can't always find the time to stay outside and monitor the fun. Why don't you offer to watch the younger children for them? Setting up cool winter activities is fun and, if you're almost babysitting age, a good way to introduce yourself to parents.

Arrange a time to winter-watch the younger children in the neighborhood. Charge an admittance fee for each child. Mark each activity station by coloring a patch of snow with food coloring or colored juices.

Frosty activity ideas: (a) *Ice tower.* See who can stack ice-cubes the highest. (b) *Snowball pitching.* Build a target to hit or try knocking over tin cans. (c) *Snowman decorating.* Give out prizes for the prettiest, weirdest, and biggest. (d) *Sled count.* If you have a small sledding hill in your yard see who can make the most runs. (e) *Snowy treasure hunt.* Hide prizes or candy around the yard. Give each child a winter hat to carry the treasures they find. (f) *Snow forts.* Two teams construct a fort. (g) A thermos of (not too) hot chocolate could top off the activities.

## Suggested Revenue
- $2.50 to $5.00 per child.

## Tips
- While the children are with you, don't let them wander off, get too cold (shivering children are cold children), or play dangerously—you know, no slushballs or planting each other's faces in the snow.
- Walk each child back home safely, and hang out until he or she goes inside.

## Tools
- Great game supplies: food dyes, ice-cubes, snowball target or tin cans, winter prizes or candy, winter hats, flags, and hot chocolate with cups.

Don't freeze up when it comes to taking responsibility! Be cool about taking charge.

---

## Business by the Book—
# Be Responsible:

Luke 16:10—*Whoever can be trusted with small things can also be trusted with large things. Whoever is dishonest in little things will be dishonest in large things too.*

Snowballs are small things. Ice-cubes are small things. Kids are not small things. They're "large things." If you want to put snow, fun, and kids together, you have to earn the kids' parents' trust. Parents want to know their child will be safe and happy with you because you're responsible.

Earn their trust. Start small. (No, don't lob small snowballs at them.) Be honest in little things: Do what you say. Always do your best. Then they'll trust you with big things.

Pretty soon you'll be snowed under with kids and trust!

# 26

# Knot-by-Chance Hair Designs

Tangles! Skydivers hate 'em and mountain climbers get hopping mad. They make tying shoes and flying kites impossible. Don't let knots mess up your cool. Join the anti-tangle team. Hair braiding, wrapping, and beading will make you and your customers look fantastic.

Before a birthday party, Fourth of July, or other fun event, set up a hair design studio. You can do people's hair and teach other kids to do it too! Post advertising fliers around the neighborhood. Your studio can be inside your house or even on the front lawn. All you need is a few chairs and a card table for accessories.

There are many fun books on hair braiding and easy-to-do styles. Some even include bows, ribbons, and beads. Have books and pictures ready for your customers to browse through. You want a clear idea of the style they want so they'll be extra happy in the end.

## Suggested Revenue
• $1.00 to $3.00 per hairstyle.

## Tips

- Friends may want to bring their own hair accessories. If not, have a few items in sandwich bags for sale. Your parents can help you shop, budget, and price.
- Never use hair dyes or scissors. Leave that to the real professionals.
- Practice on your mom first. She'll love it.
- Sterilize or wash all combs or brushes between customers.
- Avoid tangles by pulling the brush or comb all the way down, and out of the hair.

## Tools

- Completely vogue hair supplies: bows, ribbons, hair bands, beads, scarves, fake or dried flowers, combs, brushes, and other hair-styling aids.
- Studio stuff: lawn chairs, card tables, cash box, cellophane sandwich bags, and hand mirrors.
- Trendy fliers: paint, felt pens, paper, ribbons, or computer paper and printer.

Don't let life's tangles get you down. When that happens, we should stop and ask God to help us find the right attitude and solution.

---

### Business by the Book—
## Be Diligent:

Proverbs 14:23—*Those who work hard make a profit. But those who only talk will be poor.*

Hum-de-dum. Wrap a braid in a ribbon. Chat a little. Braid some more. Tell a story. . . . Whoops! Where did the time go? I guess I just talked my profit away.

Talking passes the time. Talking is fun. Talking is friendly. But talking on the job slows you down. Work too slowly and your "profit" walks away with the two customers you just lost because you never got to them.

Work hard, fast, and well. Doing five hairstyles in two hours is way better than two. There's your profit!

---

# 27

# Copycat: In-House Babysitting Service

Don't look! There's something following you. It does everything you do. It sticks to you like a small shadow. It's a copycat. Do you have little copycats in your house, church, or neighborhood? Do you have little people that just love to tag along? Don't get annoyed, get busy! Start your own In-House Babysitting Service. Moms with little kids can sure use help looking after them.

When parents you know in your neighborhood or church are busy with household chores or other work at home, offer to look after their little kids for them. Not only will this earn you money, it is an excellent way to gain experience (with supervision because the parents are at home) for babysitting jobs. Make in-house babysitting a regular routine. Work out a schedule—perhaps two afternoons a week.

Keep your copycats busy by: (a) playing games, (b) fixing simple snacks, (c) doing crafts, (d) putting on a play, (e) using the computer, or (f) helping with homework. There are hundreds of things you can do together.

## Suggested Revenue
- $2.00 to $3.50 per hour.

## Tips
- Remember, you are in charge. It is your job to keep things quiet so the parents aren't disturbed.
- Make a chart and give rewards for good behavior.
- Plan out activities beforehand so your copycats don't get bored.

## Tools
- Right-on reward stickers or treats.
- Games.

Being mature and helpful in small things is one way to show your parents and others how responsible you have become. Not only will you earn the parent's respect, but with maturity and responsibility comes more freedom and rewards. When it comes to doing things right, we always have a good example to follow. Jesus wants us to be His copycats.

---

### Business by the Book—
# Plan Ahead:

Proverbs 16:3—*Depend on the Lord in whatever you do. Then your plans will succeed.*

How do you keep little tykes busy one or two afternoons a week? Tear your hair out? Interesting, but painful. Play it by ear? There's not much music written for the ear. That unplanned stuff works only for so long. Then you either run out of on-the-spot ideas, or you don't have the items you need. To have a successful business you have to plan ahead!

Brainstorm with your parents. Or the kids. Read activity books. Plan two or three weeks ahead. Pray about it. God has the best ideas! Look at what He came up with: You and the little children you are babysitting. Trust God to help you handle the kids. You'll have great fun! Depending on Him means success.

---

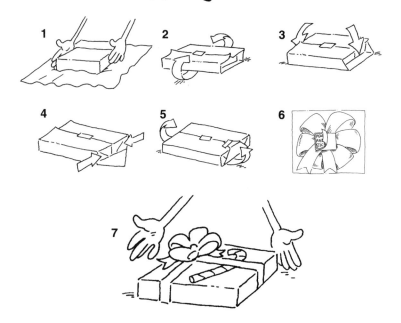

# Under-Wraps Gift Wrapping Service

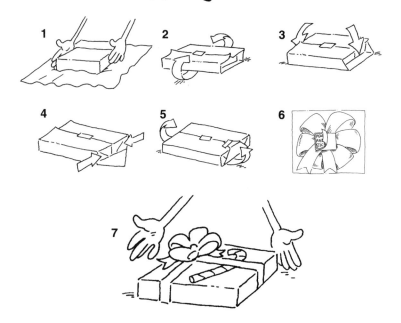

UmphwasChrismapresuntle. Sorry. This tape gets everywhere! I said, "Would you like me to wrap your Christmas presents?" A gift wrapping service is just the thing for busy shoppers.

Does your community put on a craft fair? Find out early in the fall and reserve a table. Make a few samples out of empty boxes to: (a) brighten your table, (b) show different wrapping styles, and (c) show the quality of your workmanship. Wrapping prices will depend on how much material is used, and how much time it will take you to create it. Set a size limit and charge more for very large presents.

Be organized. Customers may want to leave their present with you while they shop. Set a time for them to come back for their gift. Remember, if you're very busy it may take longer. On a small self-stick note write your customer's name and the style of wrapping paper they want. Stick the note onto the package so it doesn't get lost. Make sure you remove price tags and your note before wrapping. When you've finished, lightly replace the self-stick note on the gift.

## Suggested Revenue
- $2.00 to $4.00 per gift.

## Tips
- Time yourself and practice wrapping so you're both quick and neat.

## Tools
- Incredible variety of wrapping paper and bows. Be thrifty by buying in bulk.
- Amazing adhesive tape, scissors, and a trash can.
- Fabulous extra present stuff. Kids: balloons, stickers, and Christmas candy. Ladies: paper doilies or dried flowers. Men: pinecones or pre-made paper neckties.
- Super self-stick notes and a pen.

You want your customers to be proud of the way their present looks. Excellence in everything you do is also a gift that you can share with others.

---

**Business by the Book—**
## Set High Standards:

Colossians 3:23—*In all the work you are doing, work the best you can. Work as if you were working for the Lord, not for men.*

God loves everyone, including your customers. Keep that in mind as you work—do your best. You can't create satisfied customers by doing the bare minimum. That creates buy-once-and-never-see-you-again customers. Instead, treat each one as you would Jesus: Do your very best job for each customer.

Satisfied customers mean return customers. If they like what you do and feel well treated, they'll come back. They'll even tell their friends about your great work. Also, you'll know God is pleased. What better reward is there?

# Team-Up Construction: Gingerbread Houses

My friends and I are going to build the most enormously awesome Gingerbread house in the whole world. We're going to make a Gingerbread sky scraper, with automatic door openers, a parking lot underneath, and a working escalator. We'll win first place for sure! Okay . . . maybe we can't put in all that stuff.

If you've always wanted to be an architect, now's your chance. Many stores and community centers sponsor Gingerbread house competitions.

Most contests are advertised in your city's newspaper or on community bulletin boards. Contestants can sometimes win ribbons, prizes, or even money. If you're stumped for house ideas, study Christmas craft books, buy a kit, or even take a class. There is a world full of house designs! You may want adult help with the baking, but the rest is up to you!

## Suggested Revenue
• Prizes or prize money.

## Tips

- You can construct your house on your own or as a team. Have a "House Raising Party" with your friends and enter the contest together. Have snacks and drinks ready to celebrate the project.
- Make sure your Gingerbread is thin because it's hard to build with heavy walls. Just follow your mix or recipe directions.
- If you become an award winning builder, try selling your houses as Christmas Decorations.

## Tools

- Amazingly easy Gingerbread and sticky frosting recipe, or pre-mixed Gingerbread package and canned frosting.
- Prize winning decorations: candy, miniature doll-house items, household objects, and sturdy wood base.

Well, we didn't win the first prize or the second prize or even the third prize. But, you know, I had fun with my friends and a great time at the competition. How we handle winning or losing tells people a lot. We want to be a good witness in everything we do.

---

**Business by the Book—**
## Be a Good Witness:

Matthew 5:16— . . . *you should be a light for other people. Live so that they will see the good things you do. Live so that they will praise your Father in heaven.*

Make the right impression. Be a sparkling light.

People are watching. They're looking for honest, trustworthy business people. Let them see you living as Jesus wants you to and having fun doing it. Light up your neighborhood, school, and church.

When people know you're a Christian, they'll become interested in God. They'll want to get to know Him because of your example.

So light up and shine.

---

# Getting the Work

You're in the front row, the screen is huge, and the movie characters are as big as dinosaurs. The ad is electrifying, the sound is booming, and the special effects are heart-pounding. You just can't wait to see this movie, but it won't be in the theater for months. Stop! Think about what has just happened to you. You have just survived a mega-advertising moment. The film makers have caught your attention, and now you'll be back in the next movie line up.

A business has to have customers, or it won't make any money. One of the most important things you can do for your company is let people know about your service or product. Advertising is all around us from TV commercials to building signs. Businesses want us to know about their products or services and their advertisements are all saying "Buy from me!"

The movie companies choose movie theaters to advertise in because people who watch movies will want to go to more movies. Simple. They are potential customers or future movie watchers. As a business person, you have to decide what is the best way to let people (potential customers) know about your awesome product or service.

Advertising doesn't have to be huge, loud, and full of tricky effects to work. For smaller companies, like yours, fliers and posters will attract your potential customers. When you see big movie advertisements, they always show exciting scenes from the movie to get you interested. But how would you feel if you saw this great movie advertised, but when you went to see the movie, it didn't have any of the cool stuff you saw advertised? Nobody dove off a huge cliff, rode a killer whale, or fought alien spaceships. Nothing. Wow, what a rip-off! You would wonder what happened. And you would be right.

When companies advertise, they are promising to give you the exact product or service they show or write about. The movie company has to show you the scenes they promised in their advertisement. That's called honesty in business.

Honesty goes even further than that! What if the movie company said in their advertisement that at a special time you'd get in for half price? That means they have to honor their promise to you. Once a price is advertised, the company can't change its mind. Enjoy!

What would happen if you were watching a movie and the projector broke? Is that just too bad for you? Nope. It's too bad for the movie theater! When you bought the ticket, the theater promised to show you the entire film. If it can't do that, it has to give you your money back, or promise that you can see it at a later date. When you do business, your customers expect you to do the job to the best of your abilities. That means excellence. If you can't do the job, don't promise you can.

Advertising in business is like an adventure where you're finding lost customers, shooting the price rapids, testing the strength of your abilities by making your business be everything it should be and by being the "Honesty Hero" (saying and doing exactly what you promised). If you can trek the Advertising Adventure, your customers will come back again and again. And like any good movie it will have a happy ending with many Advertising Adventure sequels.

# SPRING

Want to join me on a Spring Safari? We can

go on a photo hunt. Grab a camera

and your bike. You can take pictures of the

things that come with the warmer

weather. Baby animals, flowers, kites, rad

skateboarders, and boats out on the water.

Remember, don't feed the skateboarders.

There are a hundred things to do

in the springtime. How about we

scout out some very serious

vocations (jobs)? Smile!

# 30

# Nature-Rave Flower Arrangements

Help! Help! Could you throw down a rope? You see I started digging a hole to plant my flower seeds, and I got carried away again. Do you love to garden and arrange flowers? This idea might just grow on you.

Explore garden books and make a list of flowers you think are interesting. Your parents can help you decide the best plants for your climate and garden. Plant seeds or seedlings in your garden or even in patio containers. If you feel like a gardening goof or agricultural klutz, collect wild flowers instead. Find a sunny meadow and spend the afternoon picking and gathering. Make sure you have your parent's permission and that it is all right to pick the flowers. Plan ahead and dry some of your flowers by hanging them upside down.

Put together a wildly lively flower stand and sell your flowers. You can make Easter bouquets, table centerpieces, garlands, wreaths, and corsages. For little girls, make pretty flower and ribbon Easter crowns. First, make a circle with thin wire. Use floral tape to secure the flowers and ribbons until no wire shows. With these easy crowns, little girls will feel like fairy princesses.

## Suggested Revenue
- $3.00 to $10.00 per creation.

## Tips
- Perhaps combine flower sales with a drink stand.
- Cut flowers love the shade because it keeps them fresh. So keep them cool and out of the too hot sun.
- Be a sweetpea by giving a bouquet to someone who may not get them often, maybe a senior citizen on your street.

## Tools
- Naturally perfect: flower seeds, seedlings, wild flowers, and leaves.
- Creation accessories: thin wire, ribbons, floral tape, large pins, and floral paper or foam.

Flowers do fade quickly so customers won't pay a kazillion dollars for your creations. Decide on a price that covers your cost and makes you money, but also makes your customers happy. Dig it!

---

### Business by the Book—
## Be Generous:

Proverbs 11:24—*Some people give much but get back even more. But others don't give what they should, and they end up poor.*

It's the little extras that make life rich: a waffle cone, a compliment, a favorite meal, a tip. It's the same with business. Give your customers a little extra—add a pretty ribbon or more flowers—and watch them smile!

Or, even better, give to people who aren't your customers. Lots of folks love flowers but can't afford them. Give someone a bouquet just because! You'll find you receive too. First, you'll get a great feeling! Then, when they love your attitude, your work, and the little extras, the word will spread.

So don't be stingy with your sweat or time. Generosity breeds happiness and more generosity. Make someone's day, and he or she'll make yours!

---

# 31

# "Hi There!" Greeting Cards

There's a bee in my mailbox, and he is real mad. I've just got to get in there. I'm expecting a birthday card, and I've been waiting for days! Giving cards is almost as much fun as getting them. Are you open to starting a card-making business?

A few weeks before special holidays, start making your cards. There are so many easy ways to create dazzling cards: (a) Stickers. (b) Stamps with colored ink. (c) Glue dried flowers, feathers, and other natural things.(d) Fancy hole punches. (e) Pop-out art using tape and paper. (f) Marbleized paper. (g) Fabric paint drawings. (h) Tempera paint prints with shaped sponges or fruit slices. (i) "Stained glass" cards with tissue paper. (j) Funny animation figures with felt pens or by computer. Let your imagination go card crazy.

## Suggested Revenue
• $1.50 to $3.00 per card.

## Tips

- Search craft books or stationery and craft shops for easy, inexpensive ideas.
- Get permission to sell your cards at flea markets, craft fairs, school or church activities.
- Advertise! Pin your cards on a cork board as display samples.

## Tools

- Big variety of art supplies: plain, computer, tissue, and construction paper; pens, pencils, stamps, ink pads, and hole punches; feathers, dried flowers, glue; stickers, tape, fabric paint, tempera paint. . . .
- Easy-to-move display board with colorful tacks.

I got my birthday card! Sometimes it's hard not to be impatient for things we want. Impatience can lead us to feel sad or frustrated. God wants us to be content with who we are, the things we are doing, and the many things He provides us.

---

### Business by the Book—
# Budget:

Proverbs 21:5—*Those who plan and work hard earn a profit. But those who act too quickly become poor.*

Don't act too quickly—poverty's a lousy goal. Profit's a better goal. So make a plan and budget! Look at the money you have and the supplies you need. Plan the best way to spend your money. Then only buy the things on your plan. That's a budget. Simple.

Don't spend more than you have. Let's see: advertising supplies, card-making stuff—paper, pens, stickers, stamps. . . . Wow! Look at that stamp! I've got to have it. . . . Oops, out of money. It will have to wait. Sell some cards, then buy the special stamp.

A budget's no good if you don't stick to it. Work your plan. You'll earn a profit.

# 32

# Clean-Up-Your Act-tic: Operation Organization

On guard, you spider webs, dust bunnies, and clutter monsters! I've got my feather duster, and I'll use it if necessary.

Do you have spots in your house that nobody seems to have time to tidy up? Attics, basements, garages, and tool sheds can be adventures waiting to happen. Suggest to your parents or grandparents that you'll tackle these lost worlds in exchange for money, treats, or other surprises.

All right, Commander Clean-Up. Prepare your operation. Make a cleaning battle plan and get going! Before you start, make a list of which items are to be kept and which items are to be thrown out. Carefully sort items into piles. Put away and reorganize the kept items. Double check and remove unwanted items. Lastly, clean up the area. There'll be dust, dirt, and creepy stuff, but you're tough.

## Suggested Revenue
- $4.00 to $5.00 per hour.

## Tips
- Strategic information! There may be a hidden bonus for all your hard work. Sometimes parents and grandparents have some pretty cool old stuff they don't want. Ask if you can take a few things for your fort, dress-up clothes-trunk, or room. After all, what's an adventure without buried treasure?
- Ask an adult about which cleaners to use on what things, and don't ever mix cleaners together.

## Tools
- Operation Clean-Up's equipment: workman's belt, mops, brooms, boxes, dusting rags, paper towels, garbage bags, floor cleaner, glass cleaner, and wood polish.
- Generous bonus: one free air freshener.

When you work for other people, they're the big boss, the ultimate commander, and the all-around important person. Do the job exactly the way your employer wants it done!

### Business by the Book—
## Serve Others:

Matthew 10:24—*A student is not better than his teacher. A servant is not better than his master.*

. . . A Commander is not better than his Admiral. So, Commander, you have to follow orders. "Yours is not to question why, yours is but to serve and . . . fly?" The point is, when you're hired to do a job, you're hired to *serve* the customers to the best of your ability. The customers take on the role of Supreme Ultimate Boss Admirals. That means you do what they want—not what you think is best.

Serve your customers willingly. Smile. Salute. Let them know you *want* to serve them. Make them feel special and respected. You'll have happy, satisfied customers. And you'll be in line for a promotion! Oh, what a great feeling!

# 33

# Piece-of-Cake Bake Sale

What a dream! I was snowboarding on a double chocolate chip cookie down a slope made of hot fudge. Wiping out was an awesome experience! If you live for major cookie action, try this bake sale idea.

Don't worry, baking is easy—with a little help and a cookbook. Ask if you can set up a bake stand in front of your house. Hint: maybe do it at the same time as your parents are having a garage sale. If they say yes, post signs to advertise and, with an adult supervising, bake, bake, bake.

For extra fun, organize a cakewalk. Cakes and plates full of treats make delicious prizes. Each prize should have a secret number between one and twelve. In a big circle on the ground tape twelve numbered sheets of paper or draw numbered squares in chalk. Charge each person an entrance fee for each round played. Try to get twelve people for each round. Have each person stand on a numbered square. Play music and have them walk from square to square like musical chairs.

When the music stops, the players freeze on a number. The person standing on the matching secret number wins. Clear the cake walk for the next group of paying customers.

## Suggested Revenue
- $3.00 to $5.00 for baked goods; $0.25 to $0.50 per cakewalk.

## Tip
- Bake sales and cakewalks are great ideas for charity events too.

## Tools
- Hot stuff: good recipes or favorite pre-packaged mixes, baking goods, decorations, pans, oven, and other important kitchen things.
- Game parts: chalk, paper, tape, felt pens, music tapes, and tape player.

An opportunity is making the best out of a situation. Combining a bake sale with another event helps both activities. Hey! Kind of like combining snowboarding and hot fudge.

---

### Business by the Book—
# Be Honest:

Proverbs 11:3—*Good people will be guided by honesty. But dishonesty will destroy those who are not trustworthy.*

Don't be destroyed by "little" dishonesties. Don't "forget" to pay your parents for the ingredients you use. Don't charge too much, "fix" the prizes, or give wrong change. . . . Little dishonesties lead to big ones. And, whoops, there goes the business! No one returns to a cheat.

Honesty takes guts. It means paying up, returning extra change, admitting a mistake, and perhaps even losing a bit of money. But if you want to succeed, business honesty is a must.

Be guided by honesty. Customers will love you. And, they'll line up for your great product or service!

---

# 34

# Sale–Away Assistant Manager

I'm under here! Under this pile of stuff. See my hand? I opened my bedroom closet and an avalanche of old toys hit me. Do you have the same problem? Ask your parents if your family could have a spring garage sale. Your folks can help you find out the regulations in your area for having a sale— like fees. Suggest you'll clean out your room, garage, and attic. Organize the event for a percentage of the money you'll make at the sale. Now that's a very tempting deal!

Next, Disaster Zone Rebuilding! Clean out storage areas and divide items into garbage and sale piles. Remember, people want to buy used items, not completely-demolished-so-not-even-the-dog-wants-to-chew-on-them items. Price and label items for sale.

Price fairly! For example, nobody will pay two dollars for a headless action figure. Have your parents go over the pricing with you. Advertise the sale by placing an ad in the classified section of the paper or by putting up bulletin board notices and banners or signs along the roadside. (Make sure you know the local regulations for banners too.)

Early in the morning, neatly set up the items for the sale. Be sure they are not cluttered or dangerously stacked. When people arrive, wait on customers and handle sales. Remember: be helpful, not pushy. At the end of the day, count up the money. Then pack unsold items for straight-back-to-storage or to give to a charity.

## Suggested Revenue
- Whatever you make at the sale.

## Tips
- Bargain hunters may ask for a lower price than what's marked. Check with your parents before agreeing to a different price.

## Tools
- Assorted used stuff.
- Neon price-tag stickers or masking tape, and a marker.
- Cashier table and money box.

Being good in business and treating your customers fairly is important, but don't stop there: Treat everyone fairly.

### Business by the Book—
# Honor Authority:

1 Peter 2:13—*Obey the people who have authority in this world. Do this for the Lord. Obey the king, who is the highest authority.*

No kings around? Don't worry. There are plenty of authorities to give your obedient allegiance to: parents, teachers, bosses, clients. . . . Who are your garage sale monarchs? You guessed it: your parents. It's best to honor and treat them with respect because they're in charge. God makes people "kings" and bosses on purpose. Their responsibility is to lead. Yours is to honor and obey them. So handle the garage sale their way.

Authorities, starting with God, tell you to do things a certain way because they know that way will work out better for you. Honoring and obeying them is just the smart thing to do. It can put you in line for business stardom. Or how about a throne?

# 35

# Dog-Run Pet Wash

Heel! Sit. Through the hoop. Good boy. Hi! I'm busy training my performers for my peewee circus. Well, fleas have to earn a living too, you know. You can put fleas out of the dog business by running a Pet Wash. Do you own a dog or have friends and neighbors who do? How about you and a partner bathing dogs one sunny afternoon?

Write up a notice announcing your dog-washing service. State a day, time, place, and price. Make a list of dogs and owners you know well. Drop off your notice at their homes a few days before your pet wash.

On the day, set up lukewarm tubs of water in a sunny location. Bathe each dog separately and work the shampoo thoroughly into the hair. Remember, don't get shampoo around the eyes. Rinse and dry the dog completely, and change the water after each dog's bath. With the owner's permission, give each pet a doggie treat for being so good. It's a nice idea to keep a water dish ready for thirsty dogs, too.

## Suggested Revenue
• $2.00 to $4.00 per wash.

## Tips

- Never bathe a dog you don't know.
- If the dog wash is a success, do one every few weeks during the spring and summer.
- Be kind and careful with dogs afraid of water. If water panic sets in, don't bathe them.
- Every pet should be on a leash. And keep animals away from each other.
- No tub mixing. Bathe one animal at a time.

## Tools

- New and improved dog shampoo. Ask a pet store to recommend a good all-purpose dog shampoo.
- Tough tub stuff: bath tubs and small containers for wetting and rinsing.
- Tuggable towels. Make sure they're old!
- Lip-slobbering doggy treats. Remember they're for dogs!

Having a pet means taking on a big responsibility (stewardship) and that takes commitment.

---

### Business by the Book—
# Be Diligent:

Proverbs 12:24—*Hard workers will become leaders. But those who are lazy will be slaves.*

Leader of the pack—that's where you're headed. Work hard and be the head, not the tail. Who wants to end up slaving away for a pack of doggy types (people who are growlers or don't know how to work)? No, better to have them panting at your heels.

Diligence in any job pays off: Work fast. Work smart. Don't waste time. And do a bang-up job. These diligence keys make your services worth more, which leads to bigger jobs with more responsibility. God will be pleased. Your customers will happily wag their doggy-tails. Their owners will smile. Your bank account will overflow. And you'll feel great!

Diligence is the way to lead!

---

# 36

# Two-Tire Tune-Ups

Ssssh. This is a very delicate procedure. Give me pliers and screwdrivers. There! I, Doctor Richmond Gear, have successfully removed a broken ball bearing. Just joking. I'm not really a doctor. But, if you're the mechanic with the most, try starting your own neighborhood bike tune-up service.

Before your business opens, be sure you already know a lot about bikes. Talk to bike clubs, experienced cyclists, or mechanics at your local bike shop. Go to your library and read up on bike repair. Practice your new knowledge on your own bike.

Make a sidewalk sign and set it up a week before you open. List times, prices, and services such as tire pumping, patching, and changing. Bike washing and chain or gear oiling are easy too. Set a time, say every Saturday morning between ten o'clock and noon. It might take a few Saturdays for customers to catch on. In the meantime work on your family's bikes. This gives you practice and attracts customers.

Set up a work space on your driveway or in your garage. Keep it neat and have a separate spot for bike washing so your work space doesn't get damp.

## Suggested Revenue
- $5.00 to $7.00 per hour, not including parts.

## Tips
- Clean up your tools and your workshop. If you leave tools around, the management (Mom and Dad) might close the shop.

## Tools
- Bold sign material: plywood, metal hinges, brush, and paint. Your sign needs to be strong because you'll be using it a lot!
- Too-cool bike tools like screwdrivers, pliers, wrenches etc., and washing equipment.
- Shop setup: chairs and tool bench or card table.

Customers trust you to do the mechanical work you promised, and to do it well. That's called doing a great job! "Don't leave home without it!"

---

### Business by the Book—
## Define the Job Clearly:

Proverbs 12:22—*The Lord hates those who tell lies. But he is pleased with those who do what they promise.*

"You promised me a new chain". . . "I meant I'd grease your old one 'til it was like new". . . A lie? A misunderstanding? Confusing misty mental moments like this can fog in a job site. Don't wait for the foggy confusion to arise. Tell people clearly what you will and will not do. Make sure they understand. Write it down so everyone and everything is clear. Have them sign it. A promise is a debt, so make sure you deliver exactly what you said. Then do a little extra.

Happy customers make happy businesses. A fog-free job site means clear cycling.

# 37

# Buzz-Cuts Lawn Mowing and Garden Service

My friends said I couldn't cut my own hair. Well, I'll show them. A little off the top and trim along the sides. Maybe use the clippers! And there you have it; one awesome haircut. Oops! Maybe I cut a little extra off. Can I borrow your hat for, say, a year? Speaking of cuts, lawn mowing and weeding are good ways to make steady money during the spring and summer.

Right after your snow removal service melts away, send out fliers announcing that you are offering lawn care. Remember, include all the right info: name, phone number, prices, and services. Keep a calendar ready. When customers call, write down which days of the week and times your clients would like you to come. This makes it easy for you to keep track of several customers over several months. You want to be extremely reliable.

## Suggested Revenue
- $5.00 to $7.00 per hour.

## Tips
- Give yourself an edge over the competition by adding a Steady Customer Summer Vacation Lawn Watering Service. For an amazingly small extra fee you'll water their plants and lawn while they are away. Hint: add that to your flier.

## Tools
- Mega powerful tools: lawnmower, clippers, edge trimmers, and rakes. (Take total care: tools may be sharp.)
- Durable: garbage bags, water hose, and watering can.
- Intelligent: plant identification book and your brain.

Generosity in business means you do that little extra work that people don't expect. It will make you stand out both as an employee and as a person.

---

### Business by the Book—
# Be Fair:

Proverbs 21:15—*When things are done fairly, good people are happy, but evil people are frightened.*

Want to put a scare into nasty people? Be totally fair! They hate that. Fairness means everyone is treated the same. Also, bad people pay for their badness, and good people get good rewards for their goodness. Sound fair? Goes for businesses, too.

A fair business charges what the product or service costs, and a little extra. Decide what your time or the job is worth. What's the going rate? Is it fair? Charge per hour or per job—charge more for larger lawns.

When you give people a great deal, they smile. A fair price for a top quality service is a happy-maker. And guess what? Your fairness reward will be seeing them again—return customers! That'll scare the unfair competition!

---

# 38

# Kids' Krazy Kites

Somehow I got my shoelace tangled in my kite string. You could kind of say I was "running" a kite making business. Get it? You can too. It's easy.

Do your brothers and sisters get bored during Spring Break? What about the neighborhood kids? How about organizing a Kid's Krazy Kite activity day? Parents would sure appreciate it and may be glad to pay you for the help.

Kites can be a breeze to make. Whether they are simple paper bag kites or slightly more complex paper kites, you are sure to find a type that matches your experience level. There are many kite making books on the market, and kite stores may have some suggestions too. Remember, don't make it too hard for younger children. Cut a kite shape out of sturdy paper, tie on a tail, and attach a string. There you have it. Now, go fly a kite!

Organize the craft supplies and working space. Allow for extra paper in case of accidental rips and tears. Set aside the entire morning for kite construction and decorating. In the afternoon take a picnic lunch outside and spend the rest of the day flying your new kites.

## Suggested Revenue
• $7.00 to $12.00 per kite each child makes.

## Tips
• Never fly kites near trees, and especially not near electrical lines.

## Tools
• Aerodynamic kite supplies: paper, scissors, rulers, wood dowels, kite string, tape, glue, paint, felt pens, and ribbon.
• Impressive self-made, packed, and ready-to-be-eaten picnic lunch.

String tangles and kite crashes are part of the fun—so, don't forget to be patient with the kites and younger children. Remember, God is always patient with us even when we make mistakes.

---

**Business by the Book—**
# Be Reliable:

Numbers 30:2—*A person might make a promise to the Lord. He might promise to do something special. If he does, he must keep his promise. He must do what he said.*

"Your word is your bond." "A promise is a debt." "Actions speak louder than words." You've heard the sayings. Know what they mean? Simple: To strike gold with people you have to match actions to words by doing what you say.

Want to change your mind? Don't *feel* like doing it? Tough! You made a promise. People are counting on you. If you disappoint them, they won't trust you again. Your reputation will be dust. So put those feelings aside and *just do it*. Be reliable. Go for a golden reputation. It feels great and shines up so . . . golden!

---

# Tracking Your Money

I learned something today. It is impossible to play a baseball game with just one person on your team. You can't slide into home and run for first base at the same time. Some businesses are like a team. They just don't work with one person.

A coach of a sports team has to decide how many players he needs and what positions they will play. You don't need three pitchers, but you may need more outfielders. A good business manager must decide how many people he needs to run his business and what jobs they do best.

A coach keeps careful track of the number of games his team has won or lost because he needs to know if they will make the play-offs. A business manager keeps track of how well the business is doing, how much of a product to make, and what the buyers want. A manager also decides how much it costs to make the product or service the company is selling.

Say it costs you ten cents to make one glass of lemonade. Why? Because you had to buy lemons, sugar, and paper cups. Every time you make a glass of lemonade you use up ten cents worth of those things. A squeeze of lemon, pinch of sugar, and a paper cup all equal ten cents. Do you charge ten cents a glass? No, no, no! Why? Because you wouldn't be making any money. You'd just be covering (getting back) the amount of money you spent on your supplies. Don't forget, you also want to make sure your business is spending your time, as well as your money, wisely. Hmmm. Very interesting. Now, sit down and decide what kind of profit (money) you want to make.

## Supplies + Employees + Profit = Cost to Customer

Say you decide you want to make 30 cents on each glass of lemonade. So! Super supplies worth 10 cents + 30 cents for you = an amazing 40 cents! You charge 40 cents a glass. You have just made an awesome 30 cents profit on each glass of lemonade sold.

What if you promised to pay your little sister 20 cents for scooping out lemon pits? To pay your employee (psst, that's your little sister) you have to charge a little more for your lemonade. Super supplies worth 10 cents + 30 cents for you + 2 cents for your sister. You now charge 42 cents a glass. You still make a 30 cent profit on each glass and after selling ten cups of lemonade you will have paid your sister her twenty cents.

Important Point Alert! If your parents paid for the lemons, sugar, and paper cups, pay them back. Paying your bills is *important.*

Keeping careful track of your money doesn't have to be confusing. You can use the "What to Charge" form in the back of the book. Filling out the form will help you plan how much to spend on supplies and how much you need to sell to make your profit. Think of it as keeping score during a championship baseball game. If you spent 10 dollars on supplies and paying employees, but you only make 5 dollars selling lemonade, when the game whistle blows the score is 10 to 5. You've lost 5 dollars and that makes you the loser. But, if you spent 10 dollars on supplies and paying your employees, and you made 20 dollars, you're the winner! Yes, you, smart business person, have made 10 dollars. Now, run around like a home-run crazy maniac to celebrate!

# GROUP BUSINESS

We're like a pack of wolves,

a herd of charging wildebeest,

a swarm of bees, a pod of whales,

and a hunting pride of lions.

Watch out! We're . . . a group

business. What's a group business?

It's people joining together to

get a job done. Now check out these

crowd-pleasing companies.

# 39

# Playing-Around Productions

To act or not to act, that is the question. Why don't you get a group or company of actors together and put on a play for a party, church event, or school talent show?

You could write your own original script (story), or use a written play or Bible story. After the script is written, the director (the person in charge) auditions actors for the different roles. When everybody has a part or character you can start rehearsing the play.

Everybody can't be actors. There are all kinds of backstage things to do like advertising, snack sales, or making the sets, costumes, and props.

By opening night or day everything should be ready. With stunning actors, costumes, makeup, sets, and stagehands handling props, lighting, curtains, and sound effects, it will be a wonderful performance. Don't worry if you're a little nervous. That's normal.

If live theater isn't for you, use a video camera and make or direct your own movie. After your movie is taped and edited, make your house into a movie theater and have a premier showing.

## Suggested Revenue
- $0.50 to $2.00 per ticket.

## Tips
- Have your movie premier at night. Decorate your house with balloons, streamers, and waving flashlights. Get your audience to dress up for the showing.

## Tools
- Dramatic stuff and whatever else the director wants.

Stories, plays, and movies are an adventure both to make and to watch. Do the best job you can do, and then take a bow.

---

### Business by the Book—
# Trust God:

Proverbs 3:5—*Trust the Lord with all your heart. Don't depend on your own understanding.*

Props in place? Costumes correct? Sounds smooth? Lights lit? Raise the curtain! Oops, forgot your lines! *Where's the prompter?*—Feeling overwhelmed? Not sure it will all come together? Relax and let the Big Director take care of it. (Psst, that's God!)

Do your best and don't forget to trust God. He has it under control. And not just your production—He takes care of all life's details *and* the big picture stuff. You're not on your own. What a relief! God can be your perfectly patient prompter for life's lines. Trust Him with your heart, your lines, your hopes, your business, your . . . everything! You can depend on Him!

# 40

# Animal Show-Offs

Do you own an Australian emu, a sixty-foot South American boa constrictor, or just a small house-broken African hippo? If you like all kinds of animals, organize a pet pageant.

Send out pageant entry forms to friends who have pets in your church, school, or neighborhood. Ask them to pay a small entry fee to enroll their pets in your pageant. Teachers, ministers, or other impartial people can be your judges. Offer trophies and prizes to the winners. Invent different categories: (a) Majorly Great-looking Cat or Dog. (b) Out-of-this-world Obedient Dog. (c) Most Kaleidoscopically Colorful Bird. (d) A+ Pet Trick. (e) Surprisingly Smart Rodent. Make a maze and time your contestants' pets through it. (f) Dinosaur-coolest Looking Reptile.

Make sure there are plenty of adult helpers to assist in the pageant. For younger children, you could organize a stuffed animal pageant with prizes for: (a) largest, (b) softest, (c) smallest, (d) hairiest, (e) most unusual, and (f) most life-like.

## Suggested Revenue
- $1.00 to $5.00 per entry.

## Tips
- Make sure all the animals are on leashes or have sturdy carrying cages.
- Keep different types of animals in different areas. You don't want fights or unexpected meals.
- If a pet seems sick, scared, uncomfortable, or aggressive, excuse it from the pageant. Remember, this should be fun for the animal as well.

## Tools
- Pageant parts: entry forms, trophies, prizes, animal snacks, maze, judges, and show rings.

Don't raise a stink by picking favorites. Remember, you and the judges have to be honest and fair to all contestants. So you be the judge of fair play.

---

## Business by the Book—
# Be Totally Honest:

Proverbs 10:9—*The honest person will live safely. But the one who is dishonest will be caught.*

Want to be safe from angry aardvarks, furious felines, irate iguanas, and frustrated friends? Take refuge in honesty. You'll be safe with the truth: No favorites is the right path. No fudging results is the key that fits.

Simple? Nothing easier than total honesty? Well, honesty can be tough, but it is worth the effort. Remember, tell the truth in love. Be tactful and gracious. Don't hurt people's feelings. An honest pageant is a fun pageant. Make your pageant pleasant for people and pets, and they'll play well and have a great time! And they'll be back.

Be honest and live safely with all manner of beasts!

---

**41**

# Cruising Carnival Caper

Step right up. A winner every time! Test your skill! Win a business! You can do it! You can organize a carnival for your church or school!

Get a group of hard-working carnies. That's carnies not Barneys. Carnies put together and take apart fairground exhibits. Carnival booths are fun to design and put together. Here are some prize-winning booth ideas: (a) Archery booth—suction cup arrows only. (b) Fish pond. (c) Funny photographs. (d) Face painting. (e) Balloon animals. (f) Dunking tank. (g) Ring and pop bottle toss. (h) Donut on a rope. Tie donuts to the end of strings and have players eat them with their hands behind their backs. (i) Darts and balloons. (j) Jousting. Have players walk a low balance beam and hit each other off with pillows. (k) The Booth of the Unknown. Have boxes of strange-feeling things and have the contestants guess what's in each box. These are just a few ideas!

Make sure you have enough people to staff each booth. Elect a Carnival Captain for each booth. He or she should be in charge of running the game, the supplies, and prizes. Have someone at a table selling Carnival Booth Tickets instead of using money. Captains can take tickets without worrying about making quick change for customers. At the end of the fair, divide the money evenly among the carnies.

## Suggested Revenue
• $0.15 to $0.50 per game ticket.

## Tips
• Dress in funny, bright costumes and use Christmas lights to brighten the area.

## Tools
• Carnival Creations: prizes and booth equipment.

A carnival is a crazy, crazy wild place! So make it exciting and fun for your customers by treating them the way you would want to be treated.

---

### Business by the Book—
# Treat Others As You'd Like to Be Treated:

Galatians 5:14—*The whole law is made complete in this one command: "Love your neighbor as you love yourself."*

Make your carnival or business a love-in. No, that's not sappy. It doesn't mean hugging everyone or fluttering your gorgeous blue eyes at them. It means being kind; not losing patience; filling the place with fun and laughter; dealing with problems respectfully; and going the extra mile . . . or three.

Sound hard? Not. Just pretend they're you and you're them. Now treat them like you'd want them to treat you. Simple. A lovin' place is the place to be. They (as them and you) will have a great time. And guess what? They'll treat you like you were them. What goes around comes around. And love's a great go-arounder!

# 42

# Fantastic-Flood Water Games

I'm riding the white water, shooting the rapids, and daring the falls. I'm rafting the extreme so please don't turn off my sprinkler.

Organize a wacky water day in your neighborhood. Post fliers advertising that you will be hosting an afternoon of water activities. The splash stations could include: (a) Water Balloon Toss or Dodge Ball. (b) Ice Water War. Play tug-of-war across an ice-cube-filled wading pool. (c) Distance Sliding. See who can slide the furthest on a water sliding mat. (d) Jell-O Eating Contest. (e) Gold Panning. Fill a small wading pool with sand and prizes. Use pie plates to pan for prizes. (f) Water Fight. Organize two teams. (g) Bubble Blowing. (h) Water Paint Mural. Pin a large sheet of paper on a fence or building and paint an underwater scene. (i) Fishing Pond Prize Booth. (j) Musical Chairs. Place some lawn chairs under the sprinkler and play musical chairs to a recording of whale calls. (k) Sand Castle Contest. (l) Popsicles.

## Suggested Revenue
- $2.00 to $5.00 entry fee.

## Tips
- All the players should bring bathing suits, towels, sun glasses, and sun screen.
- One to two hours should be plenty of water soaking fun.
- Set up each booth, and then take the water-kids around in small tour groups.

## Tools
- Watery stuff: balloons, wading pools, ice-cubes, rope, water slide mat, bubble wands and bubble soap, coins, paper, paints, toy fishing pools and poles, treats, chairs, sprinklers, nature tapes, tape player, and popsicles.

Most of these splashing games use things from around your home. If you do buy extra things, make a shopping list to avoid the urge to buy things you don't need.

## Business by the Book—
# Spend Wisely:

Luke 15:13–14— . . . *The younger son . . . wasted his money in foolish living. He spent everything that he had. Soon after that . . . there was not enough food to eat anywhere in the country. The son was hungry and needed money.*

Foolish living can look like fun: anything you want right now! Bigger, better, more! But then what? Less, less, less. The fun becomes hunger and rags.

It's silly to spend like there's no tomorrow, right? Foolish, in fact. If you've figured that out, you're smarter than the average spendthrift! Much better to be wise: budget your money, give to God and to needy people, plan what you need, spend what you plan, save for that special thing, save for college. That's wise living!

And have fun! Today . . . and tomorrow . . . and next week . . . and forever.

# 43

# International Invitational—Potluck

Italian, Greek, Chinese, Mexican. Eating different types of food from around the world is fun! Why don't you organize an international potluck? Ask your friends if they would like to manage a restaurant for one evening. Each person will create a country's traditional dish at home and bring it to the potluck.

First, make a list with each person's name, and a country's dish each can bring. Make sure you have a good variety of dishes. Decide how large a dish each person should bring. Remember, you don't want a mountain of leftover food. This is an excellent class, Sunday school, or social club event. Host it at school or church. Invite your parents and teachers to the dinner or lunch. Charge a modest fee.

Plan what you are going to serve before you host your night. Each kid is responsible for preparing his or her dish and bringing enough of it to the event. As the restaurateur, your group works as cooks, kitchen staff, waiters, and dishwashers. Adults should be on hand for emergencies, but the rest is up to you.

Set up your tables before your guests come. When they arrive, greet and seat your customers. Serve the food and drinks carefully and courteously. At the end of the meal have the servers collect the money (the bill). Easy!

## Suggested Revenue
- $5.00 to $8.00 per meal.

## Tips
- Eat your dinner before the restaurant opens. You won't have time later.
- Charge one price for each dinner.
- The big do's and don'ts: (a) Do wash your hands, and (b) don't sneak tastes out of pots or off spoons.

## Tools
- Tantalizing invitations.
- Delectable groceries. Your parents can help you shop and budget.
- Funky costumes related to the international themes.
- Trendy tablecloths, place settings, and decorations.

It will be hard work, but don't you think your parents and teachers deserve a delicious meal for a fair price and a cosmopolitan night out?

---

## Business by the Book—
# Good Product, Fair Prices:

Deuteronomy 25:16—*The Lord your God hates anyone who is dishonest and uses dishonest measures.*

God's not the only one who hates dishonest people and prices! Customers are right in there with Him! So . . . .

Your prices must be fair: Don't overcharge. Cover the cost of the ingredients. Getting ingredients on sale means you can charge less. But some countries' dishes will cost more to make. So, to get one fair price, add everyone's costs together, then add a bit for everyone's time and work (cooking, setting up, serving) and divide by the number of meals you're serving.

Your product (food) must be excellent: You might have to practice your dish at home just to make sure it's a totally edible product. But extra work makes the pot more palatable. And people pay willingly for particularly good food.

So work together to give your customers a good, fair, international "deal."

---

 # Service

Welcome to the biggest game show in this book! You can win fabulous prizes if you can answer the question "What is business service?" Time's up! The answer is, "Service is doing a job or making a product for someone else." But wait! That's not all!

Delivering good business service means having a positive attitude about helping people. But how? First, always be friendly, polite, and respectful to your customers. Sometimes you and a customer may not agree. Even if you feel you're right, you should do your best to make your customer feel good about his or her point of view. If there is doubt, the customer is always right.

When you are helping a customer, never become distracted. Give customers your full attention all the time. And don't forget! Do the best job you can for them. Be the "excellence expert!" *Excellence* in what we do, *excellence* in how we do things, and *excellence* in the product or service we deliver will, you guessed it, make us *excellent* in business.

Customers are not just walking, talking money givers. They're real walking, talking people too. Be nice. Surprise your customers by doing extra things to help out. Things that nobody has asked you to do but you do anyway. Shock and amaze them with your awesome enthusiasm.

Good service also means doing things on time. Waiting people are grumpy people. If you don't do a proper job, how do you think people will feel about you? If you guessed happy, you're wrong!

Our next two contestants in our game show will play "Beat the Business Clock." We will give you one hour to hammer nails into this piece of wood. Each nail hammered is worth one amazing dollar. To make your job easier you can rent a powerful monster nail-driving air gun for fifty cents a nail. Contestant number one, Stanley Strongarm, decides he doesn't want the machine. He wants to make the whole dollar for each nail. After one hour, Stanley's muscles are sagging and his head is aching. He has hammered an awesome 238 nails at about fifteen seconds a nail, making $238. Contestant number two, Clancy Clevermath, figures he will use the nail machine. He hammers an incredible 594 nails at about six speedy seconds a nail. But because he rented the machine he only makes $297 dollars.

Stanley is strong, worked hard, and liked the idea of a whole big dollar a nail. Clancy did some smart figuring and knew the machine would work faster and harder for him even though he had to pay for it. His fancy figuring paid off. So you can work both harder and smarter.

Diligence in business is the name of the game. To be a winner, you have to do certain things: (a) train yourself (b) work for excellence (c) give your customers good service (d) be focused so you're not distracted (e) always be on time (f) work smarter and harder. If you can keep these things in mind whenever you work, you'll build a good reputation, and have happy, loyal customers. You will succeed in the business game.

# VOLUNTEERISM

So you want to be a member of the "Good Guy Corporation"? You have proved to us you've got what it takes. Here is the Good Guy application quiz:

(a) Are you kind? (b) Are you a hard worker?

(c) Do you like doing things for others?

(d) Do you want to learn new things?

(e) Do you like meeting new and interesting people?

(f) Are you willing to work for free?

Did you answer yes to all of these questions? Then congratulations, you are a volunteer! You won't make money, but you'll get something just as valuable.

Your volunteer service is like a tithe of your time and skills. And you'll be learning new skills that will be useful to you in the future. So you could say, "Giving *Is* Getting."

# 44

# Phenomenal Visit

What tells funny stories, makes me laugh, and likes to do things with me? It's not my dog (he doesn't tell funny stories), and it's definitely not my sister. It's my grandparents! Older people have been around a lot longer than you or me, so they've seen some great stuff happen.

Why don't you take some time to visit your grandparents or great uncles and aunts. (Or, with your parents' help, adopt a grandparent, great aunt or uncle.) A visit from you would sure brighten their day. You could talk, read stories, play games, do crafts, or just go for a walk. Talking with older people is a great way to learn about town history or your family tree.

Put together a "Tell Me" notebook. On each page ask a question you are curious about: (a) What did you like to do when you were a kid? (b) What kind of jobs did you do around your house? (c) What was the most interesting thing you ever saw?

The questions are all up to you. Now get the older people to write down their answers. (Or you can.) What they write will be with you for a lifetime. Wow! It will amaze you. Maybe if you're lucky they may have some neat old pictures to show you. Your visit will be . . . well, great!

## Suggested Revenue
• No charge. Do it just because you want to.

## Tips
• Find out if your church or school would like to host a lunch or other activity for a seniors' center.
• When visiting, have an adult go with you to help with the fun.

## Tools
• Fantastic visit stuff: games, books, crafts, jokes, laughter, and good times.

Visiting people is taking the time to do something for someone else. It's both way fun and totally interesting. Grandparents are the coolest, and maybe some of their cool will rub off on you.

---

## Business by the Book—
# Be Humble:

Micah 6:8—*The Lord has told you what is good. He has told you what he wants from you: Do what is right to other people. Love being kind to others. And live humbly, trusting your God.*

Watch out! Kindness coming through. Humility on the way. Make way for the senior folks! We often find kindness and a humble attitude in grandparents, great aunts and uncles, and great-grandparents. If you want to learn how it works, hang out with some senior citizens. Treat them kindly. Go with the humble attitude of a learner. They have whole life times of experiences and wisdom to share. But you'll miss it if you visit them thinking *you're* doing *them* a favor!

Go to learn. And look out! Fun coming through. . . .

---

# 45

# Pack-Up
# Bottle Drive

*To Whom It May Concern:*
*I've been lost at sea for weeks. Just me and this annoying sea gull named Ed. I've drunk my last bottle of Fizzy Fruity Fountain Fresh. I'm writing a message and putting it in this bottle. Please Send Help!*
*P.S. You can have the deposit money for your bottle drive.*

Bottle drives are an excellent way to raise money for sports teams, youth groups, school projects, and other charities. Drop by your local bottle depot and pick up a recycling information pamphlet. The depot will give you a list of what brand names of bottles and cans it accepts. They may provide, for a small fee, recyclable plastic bottle bags and cardboard flats.

A week before your drive, leave advertising fliers in your neighborhood. Include the date and the organization you are representing. Groups of two or three volunteers collect the bottles. Another group stays at the drop-off base (someone's garage or workshop) and sorts the bottles into types and bundles them up.

Your parents can help transport the bottles to the depot. The depot tallies your bottles or cans and pays you your deposit money, which you give to the charity you're helping out.

## Suggested Revenue
• Donate what you earn to a charity.

## Tips
• Ask people to leave their bottles by the front door for easy pickup.

## Tools
• Gallons of: bottles, cans, fliers, bags, and cardboard flats for the cans.

Without help, many charities and organizations would have a hard time staying afloat. When you raise and give money to needy causes, you are part of the rescue team.

---

### Business by the Book—
## Be Content:

Philippians 4:12—*I know how to live when I am poor. And I know how to live when I have plenty. I have learned the secret of being happy at any time in everything that happens.*

The happiness secret could be big business. Talk about a money-maker! Every person in the world would buy! But, sorry, you can't sell this secret! Everyone has to find it for himself. Wanna know what it is? Contentment! Simple. It means being confident that God will take care of your needs. No worries. No jealousy. No envy. Just trust in God to make sure you have everything you need . . . and then some.

Contentment also makes it easy to give to others. Contented, happy people make great volunteers!

# 46

# Trash the Trash

I will become the greatest scientist on Earth when I perfect my ultimate invention. My name will go down in history! My masterpiece: Trash-Off Litter Repellent! One spray and you are safe from all forms of unwanted garbage. No litter bugs will dare drop their rubbish within a hundred yards of you. But until my invention is complete, the job of litter annihilation may be up to you.

The only cure today for litter bugs is a vaccination of volunteers. We need concerned volunteers to keep our cities, parks, and hiking trails clean. You can be part of the emergency team by joining and helping at community clean-up days. Schools, churches, and other organizations may want to spend a day to clean up their local parks. Why wait for an invitation? You can help out by picking up the trash that you see every day and by not littering.

## Suggested Revenue
• A clean community.

## Tips
• Trash clean-up is dirty work, so wear old clothes and thick gloves.
• Never wander away from your clean-up group.
• If you don't recognize an object, or feel it may be unsafe, tell the adults with you.
• Take found recyclables to the recycling depot.

## Tools
• Pollution Busting Equipment: garbage bags, gloves, boxes, litter pick-up sticks, shovels, and rakes.

Not only is litter ugly, it is dangerous for children, animals, and the environment. Stick with the clean-up cure. Remember, God wants us to take care of His world, so don't mess it up!

---

## Business by the Book—
# Trust God:

Isaiah 26:4—*So, trust the Lord always. Trust the Lord because he is our Rock forever.*

While you're trashing the trash, leave the rocks in place. Rocks aren't trash. Rocks are good. In fact, rocks are *strong* (they carry a lot of weight), *solid* (the big ones go deep, deep into the earth, and they won't suddenly become liquid or gas), and *dependable* (they don't just walk away in the middle of something.) See, rocks are reliable. You can trust a rock to stay a rock. You can depend on rocks.

That's why God is called a rock. He's strong, solid, and dependable too. He won't suddenly change His mind, or stop loving, or stop taking care of you. Nope. Put your trust in God, the Forever Rock, and you'll be rock solid.

# 47

# Pet Express

If you love taking pictures as much as I do, then this idea will be just purr-fect. You can take pictures of your pet! You're not the only one who loves animals. Many older people who have moved into retirement or health-care centers used to be pet owners just like you. They sure miss having pet friends. Maybe you could run or join a "pet express."

With permission from the administrators of one of these centers, you could bring in your pets for a visit in the recreation hall. You'll get a flock of admirers. Just spend an hour letting people pat or play with your pet.

There are many organizations that have Pet-Visiting Programs for Senior Citizens. Phone your local senior community centers, Society for the Prevention of Cruelty to Animals (S.P.C.A.), zoo, or petting farm and find out about their programs. Perhaps they'd love some volunteers.

## Suggested Revenue
• A petting good time.

## Tips
- Always have an adult with you.
- If the animal is nervous or unwell, don't take it or force it to do things it doesn't feel comfortable doing. All your creature pals should be on a leash or brought in a cage.
- Take along an instant camera to take gift pictures.
- The animals should always be transported and handled in a safe manner.
- Let your pet perform some tricks and give the animal a treat for a visit well done.
- Always phone and make visit arrangements before going.

## Tools
- Valuable Visit Stuff: pets, cages, leashes, pet treats, and a camera.

Letting your pet make new friends is sharing in a big way. Be as generous with others as God is with you. Generosity can be a gift, so keep on giving it.

---

### Business by the Book—
### Be Generous:

Hebrews 13:16—*Do not forget to do good to others. And share with them what you have. These are the sacrifices that please God.*

Sacrifice Sandy at your service. And what a sacrifice! I'm purring. I'm being petted. I'm munching on treats. I'm making people smile. I'm giving people warm fuzzies. (No, not hairballs—good feelings!) It's hard work, but someone has to do it.

Giving to others by doing things like visiting seniors can be a treat for you, your pet, *and* the people you visit. Generosity works both ways: You help people, and their gratitude and happiness gives right back—what a feeling! And God loves it too!

Don't let generosity be something you *should* do, rather let it be something you *can't wait* to do!

---

# Balancing

Hey you sleepy head, get up! Are you up? On your mark, get set, go! Zoom to school . . . Zoom, have lunch . . . Zoom, more classes . . . Zoom, basketball practice . . . Zoom, home for chores . . . Zoom, wolf down dinner . . . Zoom, math homework. Zzzzz go to sleep. Zoom to church . . . Zoom, youth group picnic . . . Zoom, basketball game . . . Zoom, deliver newspapers . . . Zoom, zoom, zoom, zoom. Are you tired yet? No doubt! Are some days just totally zany, going at hyper speed from one thing to another? If you do that for too long, you run out of fuel and get sick. You have to put on the brakes every now and then and just relax. Everybody has to make equal time for work and play. Cool off those rocket skates! Stop and relax! God rested, so should we.

Careful though. Zzzzzzzzzzing too much is bad too. Goofing around means your chores, school, and work suffer. Once you fall behind in things like school, it's hard to catch up again! So you've got to skateboard that fine line between Zzzzzs and Zooms. Balance is the key. You don't want to crash on either side. You have to prioritize!

Sometimes we make things too important—like sports, friends, money, or objects. When one thing becomes too BIG . . . BIG . . . BIG . . . BIG in our lives, other things have to become SMALLER . . . SMALLER . . . SMALLER . . . SMALLER because there isn't enough room. So make your priority (importance) list: God first, then family, school, work, and play. When you get your list in balance, everything just seems to get EVEN, EVEN, EVEN. Once you get your balance, the Zooms and Zzzzs work together to make one smooth ride.

# Stewardship

Can I help you? Oh! You want to rent some gardening things. Okey-dokey. You've come to the right place. You want ninety-thousand square feet of green grass with rolling hills, assorted flowers, trees, and one perfect stream with ducks. Is that it? Let's just ring it through. The grand total for all that will be . . . zero. That's right. It's free! Consider it a gift.

Wow, a gift. Cool!

God created it all: universe, Earth, trees, animals, and us. You know, everything! So really He, like, owns it all. But God shares or loans it to us for free! So be thankful by taking care of the gifts He gives us. You know, be cool caretakers. Taking care means being wise with everything we have (God's resources and creation) and having a serving attitude while we do it.

Attitude is the way we feel and work. If it pleases God when we take care of His things in a good way, don't you think He would want us to have that same attitude when it comes to our jobs? God is top quality in His love for us and His gifts. We should do the same in the service and products we make. Being good at the job we do, and being responsible with the money we make, shows others and God that we have the right outlook. A good Christian-like attitude is a gift we can give back to God.

It would be pretty selfish to keep all the good things we get to ourselves. God's not like that and we shouldn't be either.

To show we appreciate God's love and kindness, we give to others some of what God gave to us. We can tithe by giving 10 percent of what we earn straight back to God. We do this by giving it to the church we attend. The church uses the money to help people in need. Love, generosity, and serving others are also gifts God gives us. Take care of them by giving them to others as well.

# SPECIAL OCCASIONS

Prepare yourself for the entertaining event,

the happening happening, the electrifying episode,

the playing party, the fantastic function,

the special spot, the outer-galactic occasion. You

know what I mean. Prepare yourself for

doing or going to things you don't normally do

or go to. Get ready for special occasions!

Special occasions wouldn't be special, if you got to

do them all the time. So take the opportunity

to try these special once-in-a-while great activities.

# 48

# Great Globs of Goodies!

"The ragged dog likes tropical snow storms." Answer: "The water is rather hot for frogs." If you don't understand what that means that's okay. It's secret agent code talk. (They use it so they can recognize each other. Only secret agents know the right answer. And you've just joined those who know!) You're working for Interpol. That's International Producers of Lootbags. Take off your disguise and start making goody bags.

Do you know someone organizing a party or event with prizes? Offer to make goodie bags for them. You could dress up paper bags, but unusual bags are also fun: (a) *Dinosaur Egg Bags*. Cover balloons with papier-mâché and let dry; sponge paint them; cut a flap in them; fill with goodies; tape flap shut. (b) *Camouflage Cloth Marble Bags*. Fill with marbles and candy. (c) *Spaceship Bags*. Plastic sandwich bags filled with stars and other space things. (d) *Swimming Bags*. Small net bags with water surprises. (e) *Weird Science Bags*. Plastic bottles filled with treats. (f) *Pajama Party Bags*. Use surprise-filled socks. Be container crazy!

Start taking orders. Set a price for each bag made. Write down the age and number of children, and the date, time, and theme of the party. Drop off the box of goodie bags a day before the party. With your imagination and craft smarts, your bags will be the hit of the party.

## Suggested Revenue
- $2.00 to $7.00 per bag.

## Tips
- Make a customer list with types of theme bags, goodies, and prices.
- Papier-maché recipe: Combine six cups of water with three cups of flour. Heat until thick. Cool and use on strips of newspaper.

## Tools
- Top-secret supplies: goodie bag containers, paint, pens, glue, party treats, balloons, and paper.

Are you a little low on cash? Even secret agents are occasionally caught off guard. Send a note to Money Parents (psst, that's your folks). They may give you a small loan for supplies. If you have to borrow money, pay it back as soon as you can. It's best not to borrow, but unexpected things do happen.

---

**Business by the Book—**
## Borrow Only Occasionally:

Proverbs 22:7—*The rich rule over the poor. And borrowers become servants to those who lend.*

"Cash cats rule and debt dogs drool." Don't want to be a drooler? Or be ruled by a money master? It's easy! Don't borrow. When you borrow, see, you're giving the lender power over you. You're saying, "Oh, Ruler mine, you can come take your money any time you want." If you don't have the money when your ruler wants it, he or she can take something of equal value. Like your business supplies, skateboard, new outfit. . . .

Don't want someone to take your shirt in the middle of a business deal? (Losing your shirt's bad business.) Then don't borrow unless you have a way to pay it back. Better yet. Don't borrow at all! Down with drooling!

---

# 49

# Party Patrol

You're walking the beat, checking the spots, talking the talk, and doing the thing. Rent yourself out as a "Party Patrol and Game Guard." A party assistant and game organizer is sure great backup in a house full of overly excited little party guests. Once the word is out, parents will be dialing your party hotline for help.

Just the facts. If you know of a relative or neighbor who is having a child's party, offer to help with the games, lunch, goodie bags, and whatever else is needed. Discuss with the parents beforehand what types of games they would like. Arrive early to help set up. Once the party starts, be prepared to be run off your feet. Organize and help the children play the games. Remember, the birthday person always goes first. Stay behind and help clean up too. If you work well with the children and do a good job, your customers are sure to give a glowing report to other party parents.

## Suggested Revenue
• $3.00 to $5.00 per hour.

## Tips
• You could do extra things like face painting, balloon animals, magic tricks, or clown acts.
• Find out if there is a theme and wear a related costume.

## Tools
• Party Parts: costumes, makeup, balloons, and props.

When you're patrolling the party beat, you have to be responsible. So be on time, and stay at the party until the end. God is always on time for you, so set an example for the younger kids by trying to be doubly dependable and really reliable too.

## Business by the Book—
# Be Reliable:

Ecclesiastes 5:5—*It is better not to promise anything than to promise something and not do it.*

Frenzied party parents count on your promise of help. If you don't show, the show goes on but frustration fountains and fun fizzles. It would've been better if they hadn't expected your help.

In Wild West days, all gals and fellas had to recommend themselves to folks was their word. If anyone told a lie—and saying you'll help, then not helping sure 'nuf is a lie—the word spread like wildfire: She's a liar. He's no good.

Nowadays the West ain't quite so wild. But it's jest as easy to lose trust. Better to keep your mouth shut tight than to say you'll do something and not show. People rightly count on you. Put out the wildfire—be reliable. Be the kind of person folks can count on.

# 50

# A-Mazing

It twists. It turns. It takes you in circles. It ends and it doesn't. Confusing? I hope so! It's a maze. For your next neighborhood party, family reunion, school, church, or sports event, construct an adventure tunnel maze.

Ask furniture or appliance stores if you may take their old boxes. After you have collected a wide range of big boxes, start designing your maze. With paper and pencil, sketch out what you think would be interesting passages and dead ends. Add little things to make it more mysterious: (a) Hang streamers from the roof. (b) Make some little windows. Have a person waiting outside to reach in with his hand and surprise maze challengers. (c) Make secret nooks or hidden doors where your adventurers can find treats. (d) Make holes and have black lights shining in. (e) Paint jungle or funny scenes inside the maze. (f) Have funny music playing or nature sounds.(g) Make some outside holes so maze goers can stick their faces out and talk to friendly clowns outside. (h) Place funny feeling things on the floor like sponges, pillows, mop heads, or small beach balls.

Adults may help with the construction, but the rest is up to you. Charge a small fee to enter the mysterious maze. Children will have giggles of fun finding their way out.

## Suggested Revenue
- $0.25 to $0.75 per turn.

## Tips
- An older child should accompany smaller children.
- Dress up as an explorer.
- Stamp each adventurer's hand after he or she goes through. The child with the most stamps can win a prize at the end of the event.

## Tools
- Baffling: boxes, costumes, lights, treats, tape, staple gun, and maze props.

Constructing a maze can be . . . well, confusing. So get all the advice you can from helpful adults. Whenever you start a new business, reading, asking questions, and getting answers from experienced people will put you on the right business path.

---

**Business by the Book—**
# Get Advice:

Proverbs 15:22—*Plans fail without good advice. But plans succeed when you get advice from many others.*

Don't get lost in a maze of your own making. Even great adventurers seek advice—from maps, ancient books, and experts. The Bible, that ancient book, has great advice—and a map for getting through the maze of life! And God's the map-maker.

You'll be amazed how much easier advice makes life. Adults are your experts. They'll help you see the big picture, the overall plan. Pray to the Map-Maker for help. To succeed, pay attention. Going it alone is a first step to failure. Would you go into the desert with no water, no map, and no clue where an oasis is? No way! You'd get lost, dry up, and blow away. Don't be a business blow-away. Get advice.

---

# Wrapping It Up

Congratulations! You've successfully negotiated the maze of money-making ideas! You've served people, and changed your world, grin by grin. Along the way you learned a few things. Big, important things: Principles that will help you in business and life. Principles like diligence, honesty, service, planning. . . . Principles are transferrable. That means they're true for business and for school and work and play. They can be "transferred" from one part of life to another. Especially God's principles.

**⦿ PAWS Initiation.** So, did you have fun? Did you wow the neighborhood? Fill the bank to busting? Have fun contributing to your community? Gain a whole passel of RCs (repeat customers)? (Or is that a herd of RCs? A flock? Pod? Clutch? Help me out here.)

You planned, prepared, and presented your products or service to folks—and got paid to boot. Wow! You discovered that making money is, well, work. Surprised? Naw. You knew that's why they call it "work." But you also discovered it can be loads of fun, right?

See, I told you you'd learn oodles and get even smarter than you already were! Pat yourself on the back. Treat yourself to a nice cold drink. An ice-cream cone, a bag of chips. Put your feet up. Relax. Comfortable? Good. Now let's do some serious talking.

You've passed the test. You've been accepted into a secret organization for young business entrepreneurs (psst, that's you). It's so secret no one knows its real name. Some call it CIA FBI—Children Intend to Acquire all Financial and Business Institutions. Some call it the SPCA—the Society for the Procurement of Cash from Adults. You can simply call it *Profit through Attitude, Witness, and Stewardship*—PAWS.

There are a few things you need to know about PAWS' secret code of conduct. Pay attention. It's Top Secret! The Code's guaranteed to bring customers back for more.

## 🐾 PAWS Code #1: Operations Policy—Follow the Handbook. Yup.

That's the key. What do you mean? What "handbook?" Think hard. Right, the Bible. God knows how everything works, including folks, money, and life. He designed it and put it all together. Think about it. Who knows how to run a certain business best? Or a computer? a car? The folks who put the thing together in the first place—the business owner, computer programmer, car mechanic. Why? Because they know how all the bits fit together. They know what it can do and what will wreck it.

That's like God, see. He designed it all. So if anyone knows how things work, it's Him. Then God gave us the handbook so we'd know too. That means we'll be terrifically successful when we do things His way—the Bible's way. (We'll be doghouse disasters, if we don't.) His way: be honest, serve the customers, do your best, stay out of debt, work hard, be generous . . . all the stuff you've been learning. You can't go wrong doing things God's way!

## 🐾 PAWS Code #2: Attitude Policy—Grow a Good Reputation.

A good reputation is the ticket. How do you grow one? Simple. Just follow Code #1 and do everything as if God were your client. Doing things God's way—for Him—means people can rely on you. Check it out:

- You're honest—they trust you;
- You do what you say—they count on you;
- You do your very best—they get great quality;
- You serve with a smile—they feel like royalty;
- You go the extra mile and add unexpected bonuses—they love it.

All this stuff grows a reputation. It makes you popular with your customers.

So why is this important? Well, because that's how God made it to work. And take a look at the results: What do clients do to workers they like? Hire them again. How do they treat places where they feel great? Hang out there. What happens when they trust people? They call on them for help and give them more work.

See, people know when folks think of them as just a walking wallet. And they can tell when folks care about them. Guess what? They avoid the wallet watchers. People want to feel good, to know they matter. If you do your very best for your clients because you honestly care for them, they'll come back. RCs—a business person's best friend. They'll recommend you, too. Your reputation will grow and business will boom.

## 🐾 PAWS Code #3: Action Policy—Walk in Integrity.

Integrity. Honesty. Sincerity. The passwords and the bonuses. Integrity (honesty) is important no matter what size the issue. If you fudge on little things, it's easy to fudge on big ones. You have to watch the itty-bitty places where honesty matters.

Did you borrow ingredients from your folks for your business? (Hot dogs, pens, paper, string. . . .) That's part of your business cost. You can't take stuff from your parents for free then turn around and charge your customers for it. That's dishonest. Pay your folks for what you use.

Did you promise Gary Grassgrow you'd be there Saturday morning at 10:00 to mow his lawn? What if your dad offers to take you fishing? You go mow just like you promised. That's integrity. You might be able to make other arrangements, like mowing in the afternoon. But if you can't, the commitment to mow comes first.

Or say you have only a few products left and Cathy Customer asks you to keep them for her. Along comes Carrie Client. Carrie offers you three times the money for your products. What do you do? Sell to Carrie and make a major profit? If you said, "No way! I wait for Cathy!" you've conquered Code #3. Congratulations. Integrity. It's a hard-earned, precious thing. Hang on to it!

## 🐾 PAWS Code Pay-off. PAWS' code of conduct can be tough

sometimes, but it guarantees your customers and clients will be satisfied (and then some) with your work. It ensures you'll become known as someone who's worth hiring because you treat your customers right. That's worth more than cash. *"Being respected is more important than having great riches. To be well thought of is better than owning silver or gold"* (Proverbs 22:1).

So get out there and make God and PAWS proud. Doing things God's way is good for you. It's good for happiness. It's good for character. It's good for relationships. It's good for becoming like Jesus. And it's good for business. Go for it!

# PLANNING (FORM 1)

**BUSINESS NAME:**

| SUPPLIES NEEDED | BUDGET/COST | SET-UP DATES | THE BIG DAY |
|---|---|---|---|
| **Advertising:**<br>Paper<br>Pens/felts/paints<br>Tape<br>Poster-board<br>Newspaper ad | **Advertising:**<br><br><br><br><br>**Total:** | **Advertising:**<br>Banners<br><br>Posters<br><br>Paper Ad | **Check when done:**<br><br>☐ Advertising |
| **To Create Product:** | **Create Product:**<br><br><br><br><br>**Total:** | **Create Product:** | ☐ Product Made<br><br>☐ Money Box<br>(with change) |
| **To Create Costume:** | **Create Costume:**<br><br>**Total:** | **Create Costume:** | ☐ Costume |
| **For Booth/Table:**<br>Chair<br>Table<br>Tablecloth | **Booth/Table:**<br><br><br>**Total:** | **Prepare Booth:** | ☐ Booth |
| **Decorations:**<br>Balloons<br>Streamers<br>Treats | **Decorations:**<br><br><br>**Total:** | **Practice Skills:** | ☐ Decorate<br><br>☐ Set Up |
| **Business Cards:**<br>Cards<br>Stamp<br>Pen | <br><br>**Total:** | | ☐ Business Cards<br><br>☐ Smiles |

Forms for you to copy.

# WHAT TO CHARGE (FORM 2)

**BUSINESS NAME:**

| Start-Up/Fixed Costs (from Form 1) | Variable Costs (from Form 1) | My time is worth |
|---|---|---|
| Advertising: | Create Product: | $_____/hour (5) |
| _____ | | |
| Costume: | _____ (2) | It takes me_____ hours (6) to make each item or serve each customer. |
| _____ | Number of items made/batch: | |
| Decorations: | | (5) X (6) + (4) = |
| _____ | _____ (3) | |
| Business Card: | | _____ (7) |
| _____ | | (my cost per item or customer) |
| TOTAL: _____ (1) | | |

[(1)_____ + (2)_____] X (3)_____ = _____ (4) (my cost per item)

(7) _____ + (8) _____(mark-up for profit) = _____ (9) (cost I charge to customer)

**Is this charge reasonable?_____      Will customers pay it?_____**

If it's too high, I can spread (1) over several batches (3) of products to reduce cost. If I spread it over 10 batches, for example, then my cost per item is

[(1)_____ + (2)_____] + [(3)_____ X 10] = _____ (4)

# TRACKING MONEY (FORM 3)

**BUSINESS NAME:**

| EXPENSES | | TOTAL | INCOME | | TOTAL |
|---|---|---|---|---|---|
| Start-Up Costs | Variable Costs | | No. Items Sold | X (9) from Form 2 | |
| | | | | | |
| | | | | | |
| | | | | | |
| | | | | | |

| | | |
|---|---|---|
| **Monthly Balance:** | Total Income | _____ |
| *minus* | Total Expenses | ‾_____ |
| *equals* | **Profit or Loss** | =_____ |

# CLIENT CONTACT (FORM 4)

BUSINESS NAME:

| CLIENT NAME | ADDRESS | PHONE | DATE | *DUTIES | CHARGE | **COMMENTS |
|---|---|---|---|---|---|---|
| | | | | | | |
| | | | | | | |
| | | | | | | |
| | | | | | | |
| | | | | | | |
| | | | | | | |
| | | | | | | |
| | | | | | | |
| | | | | | | |
| | | | | | | |
| | | | | | | |

* Brief description of what you do: eg. edge sidewalk or oversee games.
** Special notes regarding client's preferences or times he or she will be away.

# GLOSSARY

**Advertise:** to let people know about a business (marketing) in order to get them to come and buy a product or service.

**Bills:** the amount of money to be paid to a person or business for services or products.

**Borrow:** to obtain money from someone to use in the present, with the intention of paying it back later.

**Budget:** a plan of how much to spend and what it will be spent on.

**Business:** the offering of a service or product for money.

**Client:** person who is served or to whom something is sold.

**Contentment:** being satisfied with the present situation, and having the conviction that God will meet your needs.

**Contract:** a written agreement between people that describes what will be done, how much will be paid, and the date it will be done by.

**Customer:** see Client.

**Debt:** money owed to someone as a result of borrowing (a loan).

**Diligence:** to work hard, smart, and fast to the best of one's ability.

**Discount:** to offer something at a reduced price.

**Entrepreneur:** someone who starts his or her own business to meet a need he or she sees.

**Excellence:** to do the best possible job, and then some.

**Fee:** the price charged for a service.

**Fixed Costs:** regular, on-going costs that do not depend on the number of customers.

**Generous:** to willingly give or do extra for people.

**Giving:** donating your time, talents, and resources above what you tithe to please God.

**Goal:** a desired outcome; something you want to achieve or accomplish.

**Humble:** not proud; to think of others before yourself.

**Income:** money that is received from customers for services or the sale of products.

**Integrity:** to be totally honest, sincere, and fair.

**Invest:** using money wisely in order to have funds for future needs.

**Planning:** to set out a series of steps to follow in order to achieve a goal.

**Principle:** a standard or rule of conduct and morality by which to live.

**Product:** something made, found, or bought that can be sold for profit.

**Profit:** the money left over after paying one's bills and expenses.

**Responsible:** to be reliable; to be trustworthy.

**Résumé:** a list of your work experience and knowledge.

**Service:** work done for others; the attitude of working for others willingly.

**Steward/stewardship:** understanding that all we have and all we are come from God and He desires for us to use these gifts for His glory. (Everything belongs to God; we are managers of His things. Therefore, we need to follow His instructions.)

**Tithe:** giving 10 percent, or a first part of your income to God, usually by giving it to a church.

**Variable Costs:** costs that vary or change depending on the number of customers.

**Volunteer:** to work for someone for nothing, to offer your services without receiving payment for work done.

**Witness:** to tell others about Jesus Christ and God.

## Money Matters for Kids™
### *Teaching Kids to Manage God's Gifts*

Test your SQ (stewardship quotient). Stewardship is: (A) giving money to a church; (B) being careful with my finances; (C) recognizing that God has given me everything I have and all that I am and therefore using all those resources to His glory.

The time has come to teach our children that the answer to that question is (C). All that I have and who I am belongs to God— to be used for His glory. Proverbs 22:6 tells us to "Train a child in the way he should go, and when he is old he will not turn from it."

Have you been longing for help to be better able to impart these principles to your children? The vision of Money Matters for Kids™ is to provide the tools needed to help our children and teens understand biblical principles of stewardship. We are developing fun and innovative materials, products, and programs to meet that need. Be sure to look for the **Money Matters for Kids**™ *emblem of quality* on children's stewardship products. Visit our Web site at: **www.mmforkids.org**

We welcome your comments and suggestions.

Money Matters for Kids
Lynden, Washington  98264–9760

building Christian faith in families

**Lightwave Publishing** is a recognized leader in developing quality resources that encourage, assist, and equip parents to build Christian faith in their families.

Under the direction of Rick Osborne, Lightwave has been producing high quality materials since 1984. Among the more than 50 resources are the *101 Questions Children Ask about God* series, *The Singing Bible*, *Sticky Situations* (the McGee and Me Game), *The Adventure Bible Handbook*, *The Amazing Treasure Bible*, *The Kids' Quest Study Bible* and *Financial Parenting*, co-authored by Larry Burkett and Rick Osborne.

Lightwave Publishing also has a fun kids' Web site and an internet-based newsletter called *Tips & Tools for Spiritual Parenting*. This newsletter helps parents with issues such as answering their children's questions, helping make church more exciting, teaching children how to pray, and much more. For more information, visit Lightwave's Web site at: **www.lightwavepublishing.com**

Lightwave Publishing Inc.
133
800–5th Ave.,
Suite 101,
Seattle, WA
98104–3191

or in Canada

Lightwave Publishing Inc.
Box 160
Maple Ridge, B.C.
Canada V2X 7G1